KARLI PHELPS

WHAT IS THE BIBLE?

**an interactive crash course
on the Good Book**

WINTERLIGHT
MEDIA

Winterlight Media
Zimmerman, Minnesota 55330

What is the Bible: an interactive crash course on the Good Book
Copyright © 2019 by Karli Phelps

ISBN-13: 978-0-578-60238-7
Library of Congress Control Number: 2019918263

Cover Design: Dan Peters Design

Author Photo: Clint Haley, Along the Path Productions

For JS, whose honest questions, courage, and joy
propelled the writing of this book

Table of Contents

Introduction

Growing up in church, I heard all the essential Bible stories at an early age. We memorized verses at Awana and learned about Jesus via flannelgraph. In Sunday School, we sang "God's love is like a circle" and "Jesus loves me, this I know, for the Bible tells me so."

But then I got older, and I had a lot of questions: How do I know I can believe when "the Bible tells me so"? Is God's love really unending? Is there really a God?

I started a long search for truth. I got the answers for a lot of my questions by taking classes, reading books, and picking the brains of smarter people. The more I learned, the more I saw that the evidence for the truth of Christianity was overwhelming. But at some point, I still had to make a choice: Do I believe in God, or not? And if I do believe in God, do I really believe He loves me?

Slowly, I realized that the very first verse I ever memorized back at age six had become my perspective on life: "For God so loved the world that he gave his one and only Son, that whoever believes in him shall not perish but have eternal life."[1] I chose to believe that He exists and He loves me, and that He proved it by sending Jesus.

When I crossed that line of faith, I entered into a relationship with God. But that was only the start to my journey! I found that just like in any other relationship, where you grow in knowledge of the other person over time, my relationship with God needed to grow. The

---

[1] *John 3:16 (NIV)*

Bible calls that "seeking" God; it's intentionally growing in knowledge of Him. Not knowledge ABOUT Him, like textbook information about the U.S. presidents or the Great Barrier Reef, but knowledge OF Him, the intimate knowing of an actual Person who wants a friendship with you. And God says, "You will... find me when you seek me with all your heart."[1]

This book is designed to help you as you seek God with all of your heart. My prayer is that you, too, will choose to believe that He exists and that He loves you. As you dive into Scripture, you'll see that love woven through every story in the Bible, and You WILL find Him when you seek Him.

How to Read this Book...

Engage. This is a chapter-book/devotional/ Bible-study/workbook/ discussion-group-guide sort of book. It's designed to help you turn your brain on as you study Scripture. You'll get the most out of it if you read with your favorite writing utensil in hand and a willingness to dig in.

Get a Bible out. With every chapter, you'll be reading a passage in your own Bible. If you don't have a Bible, go get one! Some churches give them away for free or will at least recommend one for you. Most of the verses I use will be from an NLT version of the Bible, but the best version is one you can understand.

Read by the day or by the week. Each chapter is short and can be read in one day, like a devotional. The whole book is also divided into six Parts, like a workbook or Bible study. You can set aside reading time every day or just work through each Part in a week at your own pace.

Read alone or with a group. This book is perfect for individual study, but you can also use it to guide a Bible study group! (See guidelines below). At the end of each Part, there are review questions you can talk about with friends over coffee or fishing.

---

[1] *Jeremiah 29:13 (NIV)*

Make a habit. Part 6 will equip you to study the Bible on your own. By the time you've gotten to that last week, see if you can create a rhythm of daily reading, writing, and praying. Be creative about when/where/how that time happens.

Discussion Group Guidelines

If you decide to meet with a friend or a group to talk about what you're learning, you'll get so much more out of your studies! Agreeing on the following guidelines will create rich and meaningful conversations.

1. Work through each Part on your own before meeting together.
2. Invite God to join your discussion by praying before you start.
3. Agree to respect each other, to listen well, and to keep confidentiality.
4. Encourage each other in faith! Learn each other's stories, pray through pain, and celebrate joys together.

DAY 0

SEEKING GOD FIRST

> Day 0 explains why daily time with God is so important. It doubles as a preview of what you can expect in this book.

We all have needs. When you're tired, you need sleep. When you're hungry, you need food. When you're lonely, you need people, and when you're overcrowded, you need solitude. We can't always function if our needs aren't met. Take a minute to think about the following question:

What do you need RIGHT NOW to function at 100%?

> Every day's entry will start with a question. Jot down an answer to tune in your thoughts to that day's topic.

Our bodies and minds and hearts all have needs. And our lives are often caught up in simply meeting those needs. Looking beyond basic needs often seems impossible – or just not worth it. Go to the gym? Eat healthier? See a counselor? Read the Bible? We barely have time as it is! Why add something to it?

And that's where Jesus comes in. Jesus says, "Come to me, all of you who are weary and carry heavy burdens, and I will give you rest."[1] He invites you into a relationship where you're no longer alone in all this. When you accept His invitation, you discover true

---

[1] Matthew 11:28-30

rest – not the laying-around kind, but the supernatural-PEACE kind – as you go through life.

On top of that, He also says, "Seek first the Kingdom of God and His righteousness, and all these things shall be added to you."[1] "All these things" in this verse is talking about food. Clothes. Shelter. Safety. When you choose to bring Him into your daily equation, He promises to solve for x. You will get your needs met – but in a healthy way.

What does it mean to "seek" God? It means starting each day believing that He exists, that He's always with you, and that He loves you. It's knowing that He's the reason you are alive today. The Apostle Paul tells us, "He Himself gives life and breath to everything, and He satisfies every need... In Him we live and move and exist."[2]

Seeking God means getting to know Him! And throughout history, the primary ways to get to know Him have been prayer and Scripture.

Now, "seeking God" is not just for stay-at-home-moms and introspective Instagrammers. In fact, God advises one of the greatest military leaders in the Bible that he will be successful when he commits to "...meditate on [God's Word] day and night, so that you may be careful to do everything written in it."[3] King Solomon, the wisest man who ever lived, agreed. He said, "Trust in the Lord with all your heart; do not depend on your own understanding. Seek His will in all you do, and He will show you which path to take."[4]

The prophet Daniel modeled this for us; he "prayed three times a day... giving thanks to his God."[5] Praying three times a day is a commitment for anyone, but Daniel was a slave in a foreign land where praying was against the law. He trusted in the promises in God's Word, and God came through for him.

Each day's entry explains a different aspect or part of the Bible. Any Bible verses I use are in quotation marks; their references are included at the bottom of the page in case you want to look them up yourself. Every book in the Bible is quoted at least once in this book!

---

[1] *Matthew 6:33 (NKJV)*
[2] *Acts 17:25, 28*
[3] *Joshua 1:8 (NIV)*
[4] *Proverbs 3:5-6*
[5] *Daniel 6:10*

If God's Word can back a warrior, direct a king, and protect a captive, it can surely benefit you! This is where daily, set-apart time comes in, and that's the challenge of this book. Use this book as a tool to help you set time aside regularly to spend time with God.

So take a chance. Spend 30 days and see if it really does help you like it promises. What could it hurt?

READ & EXPLORE

The Read & Explore sections will help you dig into what Scripture says about each day's topic. Read the verses in your own Bible and answer the questions to help you absorb and apply what you've learned.

Read Psalm 34:10. According to this verse, what is the result of seeking God? ª

The letters after the questions direct you to the back of the book, where I've shared my own thoughts on these questions. Check it out if you get stuck.

When can you carve out 15-20 minutes to read your Bible and pray every day? *(You may have more time available than you realize. For example, the average person spends 2 hours on their phone and 27 minutes on the toilet every day. Get creative!)*

Pray and ask God to help you get to know Him better and trust Him over the next 30 days.

We'll always end each day's entry with prayer as a reminder that the Lord is always with you throughout your day.

PART 1:

THE GOOD BOOK

the who, what, when, where, and why of the Bible

The Bible is a book of answers, not a book of questions.
It guides us in matters where the mind cannot penetrate
and where human reason leaves us unsatisfied.
Many blessings are given to those
who begin an honest search,
willing to follow the trail of truth wherever it might lead.

Erwin Lutzer

PART 1 INTRO

In Part 1, you'll learn all about what's in the Bible, where it came from, who wrote it, and (most importantly) why we can trust it. These first few pages have a big-picture overview of the storyline.

Bible Story Overview

Genesis – Deuteronomy. God creates the world, and it's good... until the first humans sin and break it. God unrolls a plan to restore His relationship with humanity through Abraham and his descendants (the Israelites). This plan involves a healthier way of life (laid out in the Law).

Joshua – Ruth. God's people, the Israelites, move into the land He promised Abraham... but they don't follow God's plan for life and end up in destruction.

1 Samuel – 2 Chronicles. God establishes a king to rule the people, and King David leads the people to follow God and live a good life. But soon they abandon God's plan again, so the kingdom splits and eventually falls to foreign invaders. God's people are taken captive and moved out of the Promised Land.

Ezra – Esther. God's people made some huge mistakes and were banished from the Promised Land. But God doesn't forget His people in captivity. Eventually, a remnant returns to rebuild.

Job – Song of Solomon. Books of poetry written by God-followers about life lived God's way. God's way of living isn't always easy, but He promises that it's worth it and that He'll never abandon the people who trust in Him.

Isaiah – Malachi. At various times in the story, God sends these prophets to remind the Israelites to turn back to God's plan. God loves His people and wants a relationship with them. He also previews His ultimate rescue plan: A Messiah to stop the cycle of sin.

Matthew – John. The promised Messiah arrives! By example, He shows the people how to live life God's way, and then dies to pay the price of sin. Good News, though: He comes back to life to set us free! Because of His sacrifice, all who believe in Him can have a restored relationship with God.

Acts – Revelation. Jesus goes back to heaven and sends the Holy Spirit among His followers. The church begins to grow and discover life under grace – and His mission is passed on to all His followers, including you and me.

WHAT IS THE BIBLE?

DAY 1

THE STORY AND THE LINE

In your current understanding, what is the Bible?

┌───┐
│   │
│   │
│   │
│   │
│   │
│   │
└───┘

The Bible has all sorts of things in it: Stories of epic battles. Love poems. Eulogies. Other peoples' mail. Legal codes. Sermons. But the heart of the Book – the core message – is the same from beginning to end. What is that message? Jesus said, "… the Scriptures point to me!"[1] All of Scripture, from the book of Genesis to the book of Revelation, points to Jesus. It's what the whole book is about.

The Old Testament shows us how much we need a Savior and tells us He's coming soon. Every book has a reference to Jesus. Even Job, in the oldest book of the Bible, said, "I know that my Redeemer lives, and he will stand upon the earth at last."[2]

The New Testament tells us, "He's here! Look what He's doing!" From these books we learn about the baby born to a virgin; that baby's extraordinary life, teaching, and love; and ultimately, His excruciating death. And then we hear, "He's alive!" and then, "He's

---

[1] John 5:39   [2] Job 19:25

coming back!" This message, the Gospel, forever altered the course of history.

The Gospel message is, "This is how much God loved the world: He gave his Son, his one and only Son. And this is why: so that no one need be destroyed; by believing in him, anyone can have a whole and lasting life."[1] The Creator of the Universe, a good, all-powerful God, loved humans, but the relationship He had with them was broken by sin. Because "the wages of sin is death,"[2] the people He created were destined to an earthly life without Him and an afterlife spent in hell. So, He unrolled a Rescue Plan to save them. Jesus was the culmination of that plan. Because of Jesus' death, we can have a relationship with our Creator NOW, in this life, and live with Him forever after we die.

That's the story we find in the Bible. And the most amazing thing about this story is that it's still happening! Every person who decides to believe in Jesus steps into the story found in the pages of Scripture. When we talk about "faith", this is what we're talking about. Faith is the belief that because of Jesus, we can have a relationship with our good God. Entering that relationship redefines and redirects your entire life. You're no longer doing life alone. You have a purpose. You have the protection and provision of the Person who made you and knows you best.

Entering this relationship requires a choice. The apostle Paul says, "If you openly declare that Jesus is Lord and believe in your heart that God raised him from the dead, you will be saved."[3] At our church, we call this choice "the line of faith"; when you cross that line, you enter into a new life.

Your challenge today is to figure out which side of the line you are on. Have you chosen to believe in Jesus? If you have, continue to seek God! If you haven't, ask yourself, "Why?" If you need to know more before you make this decision, this book is a great starting place for you. As we break down the contents of God's Word, you'll find many answers to your questions about who Jesus is, and you'll begin to discover how He can change YOUR life.

---

[1] *John 3:16 (MSG)*   [2] *Romans 6:23*   [3] *Romans 10:9*

READ & EXPLORE

Read John 3:16-17. What do these verses mean?[a] What does this tell you about God?

When did you "cross the line of faith" and put your faith in Jesus? If you haven't done this yet, what has held you back?

If you're ready, and you haven't already, cross the line. You can pray this prayer, or pray in your own words:

God, thank you for sending Jesus to make a way for us to be in relationship. I believe that Jesus is God and that He died for me. Please forgive my sins and lead my life.

Add a personal message to God. You can write it below or pray it in your heart. If you've never prayed before, remember – "the Lord is close to all who call on Him!"[1]

If you prayed this for the first time today, congratulations! You are now part of the family of God! Go tell someone about it!

If you've already made Jesus your Lord and Savior before today, pray that God will help you move to the next level of your faith as you spend time with Him this month.

---

[1] *Psalm 145:18*

DAY 2

GOD'S WORDS

If you could describe the Bible in one word, what would it be, and why?

Every person will answer that question differently. Maybe you're a new believer who has never read the Bible before. Maybe you're a life-long Christian who's read the whole thing multiple times. Maybe you're not sure what you even think about God, and all you've ever heard about the Bible is negative.

For me, I grew up reading my own kid-version of the Bible and learning about the stories of David and Goliath, Esther, Ruth, Noah and the Flood, Jonah and the Whale, Paul and Silas in prison... and on and on. As I grew up, I began to understand more about this Book and how the stories in it can change my life. I also began to understand that my first impressions of most of the stories weren't always right. The more I read Scripture, and the more I learned to listen to God's voice, the more accurate my perspective became.

Here's what I learned: The Bible claims to be God's actual words. The book of 2 Timothy says, "All Scripture is God-breathed."[1] In other words, God spoke all of Scripture. It all originated with Him. That's a pretty bold claim, and what you do with that statement changes the way you read the whole Book. Really, you have three options with what you say about this Book:

1. "It's lying, and they aren't the words of God." *That would make it evil. Throw it away.*
2. "The people writing it were confused." *That would make it crazy. Definitely don't read it.*
3. "It's true." *Read it, figure it out, and live by it.*

You can't say, "There's some good stuff in there, but none of it's from God." If it's not truly from God – and yet CLAIMS to be from God – it's either evil or crazy. There isn't a neutral position here.

No matter what you believe, no one would claim that the Bible is just an ordinary book. It's the best-selling book of all time; for thousands of years, people have loved this Book and based their lives on it. Empires have risen and fallen, but Christianity has survived, and every major revival in church history is centered around this Book. There is no other book in the history of humanity that compares to the Bible when it comes to global influence AND personal impact. The Bible has inspired, enriched, elevated, and instructed humanity for thousands of years.

The most logical choice is that the Bible is telling the truth. (We don't have time to talk about the staggering evidence for the Bible's validity, but check out the resources at the end of this book if you want to know more.) If the Bible is telling the truth, and it really is the words of God, this means that it truly is alive and powerful, and it will make an impact on your life when you read it.

The book of Hebrews says, "the word of God is alive and powerful."[2] In Isaiah, God says, "I send [My Word] out, and it always produces fruit. It will accomplish all I want it to."[3] God's Word has POWER. It gets stuff done. It's never just empty words on a page. The same God who spoke the world into existence spoke the words in the Bible.

---

[1] *2 Timothy 3:16 (NIV)*   [2] *Hebrews 4:12*   [3] *Isaiah 55:11*

Your challenge as a believer is to choose Option 3 – that the Bible really contains the words of God. That might be a huge stretch for you; it might just be a jump-start for your faith. But if the verses above are really true, and you hold God's actual words IN YOUR HANDS, engaging in this Book will change you forever.

READ & EXPLORE

Read 2 Timothy 3:16-17. In your own words, what is the Bible useful for?[b]

Of the things listed in these verses, which do you need the most right now?

What "good works" in your life would you like to be more equipped for? *(For example: parenting, respecting your boss, staying sober.)*

Pray. Ask God that if these are really His words, He would prove it by transforming your life for the better and equipping you for every good work.

DAY 3

THE PARADOX

What is your favorite Bible verse (or something from the Bible that stands out to you)?

We believe that the words in the Bible are God's words. Like you read yesterday, "All Scripture is God-breathed."[1] Scripture came from God, and through His Word we learn about who He is. But how did His words get to us?

A common theme throughout the Bible is that God partners with humans to get stuff done. He could easily do it alone, of course. But as great and all-powerful as He is, God chooses to use people (especially broken and flawed ones!) to carry out His plans.

The writing of Scripture was one of these plans. The Apostle Peter wrote, "Long ago God spoke many times and in many ways to our ancestors through the prophets."[2] God chose specific people throughout the centuries to deliver His messages to His people. In the Old Testament, they were called prophets. In the New

---

[1] *2 Timothy 3:16 (NIV)*   [2] *Hebrews 1:1-2*

WHAT IS THE BIBLE?

Testament, the apostles – people who knew Jesus personally – wrote about Jesus' life and the start of His church.

They weren't just random people writing whatever they want. "No prophecy in Scripture ever came from the prophet's own under-standing, or from human initiative. No, those prophets were moved by the Holy Spirit, and they spoke from God."[1] The Greek word for "move" in that verse is *pheromenoi*, which is the same word they use to describe a ship being moved by the wind. A ship can't move without the wind, and in the same way, the writers couldn't write without God's breath.

It's clear that he didn't just use them like a typewriter, though; the writer's personalities and writing styles deliver God's Words in their own unique style. It's clear that humans wrote the Bible... but also, God did.

What we end up with is a paradox: two truths that seem opposite but are still true at the same time. All sorts of paradoxes exist in our world. The best example is light (if you can remember back to high school physics). Light is both a wave (like sound) and a particle (like an atom). To scientists, it makes little to no sense – and yet, it's true! There are a lot of paradoxes in the Christian faith, too, because our God is beyond our finite brains: Jesus was both 100% man and 100% God; God is in control, yet we have free will; there is only one God, but God is three persons. Mind-benders, right? The Bible is another: it was written both by God and by humans.

This matters! Humans wrote the Bible. We can find out about the time period they lived in; we can learn about their perspectives and experiences. AT THE SAME TIME, God wrote the Bible. The words are true and have power and are living and active. They can change your life. When we read God's words and apply them to our lives, they change our hearts, minds, and actions for the better. God used humans to accomplish His plan of relaying His heart through Scripture.

If you have crossed the line of faith, you have chosen to partner with God to accomplish His plans. He wants to accomplish something great with you, too! That's why you matter and you have a purpose;

---

[1] *2 Peter 1:20-21*

you are an integral part of His plan in the world, an irreplaceable piece of the puzzle. And the more you learn about Him, the more you'll discover what that purpose is and begin to walk in it.

READ & EXPLORE

Read Jeremiah 1:4-8. What job did God give to Jeremiah?[c]

How did Jeremiah feel about that calling? (vs 6)[d]

What did God have to say about it? (vs 8)[e]

Think about the tasks you have in front of you today. What can you learn about God from this passage to encourage you in those tasks?

Pray Jeremiah 1:8 over yourself today: that in whatever you encounter, you will not be afraid, because God is with you.

DAY 4

THE HOLY LIBRARY

What is your biggest question about the Bible?

We all have questions about the Bible. Don't ever feel bad for having a question. In fact, questions are healthy; they mean you're engaging your brain! Acknowledging those questions is one of the most important things you can do as you read. I regularly write mine down and ask God about them. If Christianity is the truth, it won't crumble under an honest question.

One of the main questions I've heard about the Bible is "how do you get stuff out of it?" Which really means, "I've heard that the Bible changes lives, but I try reading it, and I don't get it." Honestly, I felt this way for a long time. I earnestly wanted to study the Bible, so I'd start in Genesis, work my way through all the famous stories, and then hit the long list of weird laws in Leviticus and give up. I did that many times. Once I even made it all the way to 2 Chronicles, but the long lists of dead people put me to sleep.

Then someone taught me the storyline of the Bible and explained how it was put together – and suddenly everything made so much more sense! So today we're going to look at the composition of the Bible – what's in it.

First of all, the Bible isn't a novel you sit down and read from beginning to end; it's more like a library of 66 different kinds of books. It's divided into two sections: The Old Testament (before Jesus) and the New Testament (during and after Jesus). The Old Testament section has writings of law, history, advice, poetry, and prophecy. The apostle Paul tells us, "Whatever was written in earlier times was written <u>for our instruction</u>, so that through perseverance and encouragement of the Scriptures we might have hope."[1] The Old Testament is a teacher for us; it encourages us and helps us have hope.

The New Testament has the four Gospels (which tell the story of Jesus), a history book (Acts), and then a bunch of letters. Most of the letters are from the Apostle Paul to the churches he planted, but some are to his leaders-in-training. Other letters are written by some of the other Apostles (early church leaders). These books tell the story of Jesus and the beginnings of the church. John tells us that "these [stories] are written that you may believe that Jesus is the Christ, the Son of God, and that believing you may have life in His name."[2] The purpose of the New Testament is to help us see that Jesus is who He says He is.

The Bible tells a story, but it's arranged by type of writing, not the order of events. That's why I got so lost every time I tried to read it from cover to cover! If you get to know the story told in the Old Testament, the order will make more sense. We'll go through that story in order this month.

But how does that story help us? If the whole thing is about Jesus, why can't we just read the New Testament and be done with it? Well, I've found that reading the Old Testament shows me God's story, and the story of His people, which helps me stay the course in my OWN story. The book of Hebrews gives us a long list of Old Testament stories pf people who changed the course of history through their faith, and we're told to run our own race of faith because of their example. (See Hebrews 11).

---

[1] Romans 15:4 (NASB)   [2] John 20:31 (NKJV)

As you begin to invest in this library of books, you'll run across some things that are confusing or difficult or just plain weird. But you'll also see the stories of men and women who stuck it out in faith. You'll learn about God's heart for His people, and you will come to know Jesus more and more. And the words of God will come alive for you as you continue to seek Him.

READ & EXPLORE

Read Hebrews 12:1-2. The people in Hebrews 11 are called "a huge cloud of witnesses". What are they witnesses (or examples) of? Why does that matter?[f]

Since we have all these examples of faith, what are we instructed to do?[g]

Which of those instructions applies to your story today, and why?

Pray and ask God to help you let go of distractions and focus on Jesus as you run the race of faith.

DAY 5

CONTEXT IS KING

Crack open your Bible for a minute. What book are you in? Take a second and write down what you know about that book, if anything. *(Who wrote it? Who is it written to? What's it about? Have you read it before? Is it New Testament or Old Testament?)*

You may have a ton of knowledge about the book you opened to; you may know next to nothing. When I first read some of the books, I had no idea what was going on. But I didn't give up! When something didn't make sense, I prayed, asked questions, picked a smart person's brain... and God slowly gave me some handles on what I was reading. The more you learn about something, the more you "get" it!

Think of it like this: say you found something written on a scrap of paper on the floor of a borrowed car. Who wrote it? Who did they write it to, and why? What were they talking about? With no context, how can you know what it's really about? Meaning always depends on context, or whatever information comes with the message. To avoid misunderstandings, you'll do your best to figure out as much information as you can before you do anything with the message.

In the same way, the more context you have when you read the Bible, the more accurate your understanding will be. It's very easy to pick random sentences and claim they mean something completely opposite to what the author was trying to say, but that's a dangerous (and just plain irresponsible) way to read. When you read a verse, look at what comes with it: look at what type of book it is (law, poetry, letter); look at the surrounding verses; look at the author and the audience; look at the culture. The more context you collect, the more accurate your interpretation will be.

Sometimes it's easy. We know that the book of Ruth took place "in the days when the judges ruled in Israel"[1] (i.e., during the book of Judges). Once you've read Judges – and learned how brutal this time period was – you'll appreciate the love and integrity that the story of Ruth conveys. But this story took place a LONG time ago. The people lived very differently back then, with different customs, responsibilities, and values. So don't get weirded out when a couple guys exchange shoes when making a deal,[2] or a woman tells her daughter-in-law to propose marriage by uncovering a guy's feet.[3] It's just a different culture!

My favorite example of this concept is a verse in the middle of the Old Testament law books: "Each of you must have a spade as part of your equipment. Whenever you relieve yourself, dig a hole with the spade and cover the excrement."[4] Yes, that said what you think it said: when you go #2, make sure you bury it. Taken out of context, it looks like God doesn't want us to use toilets, right? No! If we look at the context, we see that this was written to a specific culture thousands of years ago without any plumbing. And we see in the verse after it that the reason for this weird law is that God dwells with them, so He wants them to be holy.[5] (Holy means "set apart" from everything else.)

So what do we do with this? After you consider the context, see what light it shines on the meaning. God was telling THAT culture how to keep their camp clean and disease-free. By doing this, they

---

[1] Ruth 1:1 [3] Ruth 3:4 [5] Deut. 23:14
[2] Ruth 4:8 [4] Deut. 23:13

would represent God's wisdom and holiness to the world. That meaning carries over into our lives, too; we also can represent God's wisdom and holiness to the world. In fact, as Jesus-followers today we're still instructed to "be holy in everything [we] do, just as God who chose [us] is holy."[1] In the 2000s AD, representing God's holiness to the world will look different than it did in Bible times, but the heart behind it stays the same.

And this is how you get stuff out of a Book written for a culture long ago. The people and culture are different, but our God is the same; look at the heart of the message and apply it to your life.

The good news is that you don't have to be a literary and historical genius to get stuff out of the Bible. All you need to start is faith! If you have placed your trust in Jesus (crossed the line of faith), you always have the presence of God with you. He helps you understand more and more over time. He guides you to the right knowledge when you need it. The apostle Paul said, "we have received God's Spirit... so we can know the wonderful things God has freely given us."[2] As Jesus-followers, we have God's Spirit dwelling in us, and Jesus promised that the Holy Spirit "will guide [us] into all truth."[3] He will guide you as you read the Bible so you can get to know Jesus better!

You are never alone when you pick up the Bible; He's always there to help you. I've found that the more I invest, the more it starts making sense. So grab your Bible and let's practice studying the context!

---

[1] *1 Peter 1:15*   [2] *1 Corinthians 2:12*   [3] *John 16:13*

READ & EXPLORE

Pray. Ask the Holy Spirit to guide you in today's Scripture reading.

Read Psalm 131:2. The book of Psalms is a book of prayers in the form of poetry, and poetry uses a lot of figurative language (comparisons to help you understand something in a different way). What comparison is the writer making in this verse?[h]

Look at the context in verse 1 and 3: There is an "instead" at the beginning of verse 2. He is doing verse 2 *instead of…* what? What is he choosing NOT to do? Why do you think he is doing that? [i]

Look back at the question you wrote at the beginning of Day 4. According to this verse, how can YOU approach questions that you don't have the answer to (yet)?[j]

Pray that God will give you peace about your questions as you trust Him to guide you into the truth.

PART 1 RECAP

Congratulations on finishing Part 1! Take a few minutes as you have time, either now or at the end of the book, to review the things you've learned. Studies show that the more you review, the more you remember. If you're meeting with a group, you can bring your answers to your meeting and take turns sharing what you wrote.

Why is it important to read the Bible? How can it help you?

Who wrote the Bible, and why is that so important?

What is the main story of the Bible?

How do you get stuff out of the Bible? What is important to keep in mind when you come across a weird verse?

What has stood out to you the most from your readings so far? What questions do you still have?

How has God blessed your life over the past week? What do you need prayer about in your life right now?

WHAT IS THE BIBLE?

PART 2:

IN THE BEGINNING...

Old Testament, Part 1

God has not changed.
Therefore, wherever we rightly understand
His character and His ways in the Old Testament,
we are learning something true
about the God and Father of our Lord Jesus Christ,
who loved us and sent Christ to die for us.

John Piper

PART 2 INTRO

In Part 2, you'll lay the groundwork with the main characters and events that start the Bible. Through these stories, we learn all about the character of our Creator God and discover His plans for His people.

The Books of the Bible

Books covered in Part 2 are underlined in the list below.

OLD TESTAMENT

LAW
Genesis
Exodus
Leviticus
Numbers
Deuteronomy

HISTORY
Joshua
Judges
Ruth
1 & 2 Samuel
1 & 2 Kings
1 & 2 Chronicles
Ezra
Nehemiah
Esther

POETRY
Job
Psalms
Proverbs
Ecclesiastes
Song of Songs

MAJOR PROPHETS
Isaiah
Jeremiah
Lamentations
Ezekiel
Daniel

MINOR PROPHETS
Hosea
Joel
Amos
Obadiah
Jonah
Micah
Nahum
Habakkuk
Zephaniah
Haggai
Zechariah
Malachi

DAY 6

AND SO IT BEGINS...

Start with prayer that the Holy Spirit will help you know Jesus more today.

Why are you alive? What's the purpose of your existence?

I know that's an intense question for some of you, but I hope you gave it a shot. We all have an answer to this question, even if we've never given it serious thought, and the answer subconsciously directs our lives.

The first chapters of the Bible answer that question for us. Now, we aren't going to take apart the creation/evolution debate today. We're simply looking at what the Bible says and considering that it may actually be the words of God – and then seeing how that changes our hearts, minds, and actions.

Grab your Bible and open up to the beginning! Genesis 1 and 2 tells the story of God creating the world one step at a time. The last step – the finishing touch, the cherry on top of a perfect creation – was humanity. After speaking the planets, trees, mountains, oceans, animals, fish, birds, insects into existence, He fashioned humans by hand in His own image. All of creation was designed en masse, and it was good. But the man and the woman were designed at an intimate, individual level; God called them by name.

And every human since has been put on this earth for a reason. God tells the prophet Jeremiah, "Before I formed you in the womb I knew you, before you were born I set you apart."[1] God was planning on you. He knew about you in advance, and when you started forming, He "made all the delicate, inner parts of your body, and knit you together in your mother's womb."[2] This tells you that 1.) you were lovingly designed by your Creator, and 2.) you were made ON PURPOSE. You are NOT an accident.

So what is our purpose? God says, "I have made them for my glory."[3] Your very existence shows how great and good God is. This has nothing to do with what you do or how good you do it. We all have "good works" set aside for us to accomplish, but you bring God glory just by being YOU.

At the end of his life, King Solomon (the wisest man who ever lived) figured out the point of living. He says that the core purpose of humanity is, "Fear God and keep His commandments."[4] In other words: have a relationship with God! Know Him and live your life His way. Why? Because He LOVES you. He made you! God delights in you[5]; you are precious to Him[6]; He thinks about you constantly.[7]

Think about it like an inventor – Thomas Edison, for example. He is most known for the creation of the lightbulb. He designed it. He figured it out. It was his masterpiece, and he designed it to do good things. He was the one who decided its purpose.

Same thing with you! Your life is defined by your relationship with your Creator. The more you lean into this relationship, the more it shapes how you see yourself. it shapes your choices, and it shapes your thoughts. Like any relationship, those changes don't happen overnight, but once you've crossed the line of faith, the changes have already started. And God promises to finish what He started![8]

---

[1] *Jeremiah 1:5 (NIV)*
[2] *Psalm 139:13*
[3] *Isaiah 43:7*
[4] *Eccl. 12:13 (NIV)*
[5] *Psalm 37:23*
[6] *Isaiah 43:4*
[7] *Psalm 139:17*
[8] *Philippians 1:6*

READ & EXPLORE

Read Ephesians 2:10. How are humans described in this verse?[a]

It says that God planned good things for us a long time ago. What has He done for us to enable us to do those good things?[b]

How does knowing that God created you on purpose impact you? How will this understanding change the way you think, feel, or act today?

Pray that God will help you live this out!

DAY 7

SIN HAPPENS

Start with prayer that the Holy Spirit will help you know Jesus more today.

You've read that God has empowered you to do good things. What good things have come out of your time with God so far?

"In the beginning, God created the heavens and the earth"[1], and everything in them. Stars, oxygen, butterflies, glaciers, goats, amoebas, and a lot of other things… and eventually, YOU. You and the rest of humanity were the masterpiece of creation, and we were designed to reflect God's goodness and love. God looked at creation and said that it was good!

So what the heck happened? If creation started out so good, why is it so bad now? If we look around us today, we see death, fighting, earthquakes, wars, cancer, tsunamis, plagues… what happened to God's good creation?

---

[1] *Genesis 1:1*

The answer is found in Genesis 3, with the Adam/Eve/snake story. God gave a simple instruction, and they chose to go their own way instead of His way. "When Adam sinned, sin entered the world. Adam's sin brought death, so death spread to everyone, because everyone sinned."[1] Sin is any action or thought that is contrary to God's design. And when that first human sinned, it changed our essential nature from "good" to "bad" – it broke the world.

This is where all the pain, suffering, and sorrow in the world comes from. The New Testament explains that "the wages of sin is death;"[2] sin caused a spiritual death in our spirits, and the direction of the world changed from life to destruction.

The Old Testament shows the results of sin when it comes to our relationship with God. Before sin, God lived with Adam and Eve in the Garden of Eden. He walked with them, talked with them. But when the humans disobeyed, that relationship was marred. No longer could they live in God's presence; their sin "made a separation between [them] and [their] God."[3]

Here's the scary thing: if our reason for existence is found in our relationship to God, our very purpose and meaning is gone when we are separated from Him. It's like a branch of a tree. If you see a branch on the ground, separated from the trunk, you know it's going to die. It's basically already dead. A branch's whole purpose and its very life is sourced from the trunk of the tree! It can't survive and thrive and grow on its own.

Like a branch that fell away from the trunk, humans sinned and fell away from God's plan. The world was broken and set on a path of destruction. As the Creator, God was completely within His rights of just destroying everything and starting over. "But God does not just sweep life away; instead, He devises ways to bring us back when we have been separated from Him."[4] This story isn't over!

We know "the rest of the story", as Paul Harvey would say, because we're living after Jesus. But the whole Old Testament didn't have Jesus yet – and we still can see God's grace and love and redemption all through those stories.

---

[1] *Romans 5:12*
[2] *Romans 6:23*
[3] *Isaiah 59:2 (NASB)*
[4] *2 Samuel 14:14*

For the next couple of weeks, we are going to take a sweeping tour through the Old Testament to see the ways that God devised to bring humans back into relationship with Him. My prayer is that you'll come to discover just how wonderful and good our God really is, and that the truth will bring YOU into a growing relationship with Him.

READ & EXPLORE

Read John 15:4-8. Jesus is talking about grapevines here, and He says that when we produce fruit, we bring glory to God. (vs 8). How do you "produce fruit"? What do you think He means by "fruit"?[c]

What do you think it means to "remain" (or "abide", depending on your Bible translation) in Jesus? Look at verses 10 and 12 if you need help.[d]

What do you have going on right now in your life? What would it look like for you to abide in Jesus?

Because of Jesus, we are no longer cut off from our life source! We have a relationship with God through Jesus. Pray and thank God for His plan and ask Him to help you abide in Christ today.

DAY 8

THE RESCUE PLAN

Start with prayer that the Holy Spirit will help you know Jesus more today.

In what area of your life do you need God's goodness and power?

You've read that sin entered the world and broke it. Well, it got pretty bad pretty fast. Only three chapters later, "The Lord observed the extent of human wickedness on the earth, and He saw that everything they thought or imagined was consistently and totally evil. So the Lord was sorry He had ever made them and put them on the earth. It broke His heart."[1] But God found one man, Noah, who still lived the way God designed. Even though the world around him was evil and chaotic, Noah "walked in close fellowship with God."[2]

Because of how bad the world had gotten, God decided to clean house with a worldwide flood. He instructed Noah to build an ark to save animals and the human race. After the flood, God made

[1] *Genesis 6:5-6*   [2] *Genesis 6:9*

Noah a promise: He would never again destroy the world by covering it with water.

The promise God made with Noah is called a **covenant.** A covenant is a special type of promise. It's similar to a contract, in that two parties make an agreement with certain expectations and responsibilities. To the ancient world, though, covenants were far more than simple contracts. Covenants were wrapped up in a person's life and identity, similar to marriage. Your identity and lifestyle and perspective change when you've made a lifelong bond with another person.

Think about that for a second – the Lord, the Creator, made a covenant with His creation. He wrapped up His identity in this bond with humanity. In fact, He made several covenants with His people. This first one, with Noah, was unconditional – meaning there was nothing Noah could do to break the covenant. It was a promise God would carry out NO MATTER WHAT.

Several generations after Noah, God unrolled His plan to lift humanity out of that muck to guide them in a better life. In this plan, just like with Noah, He would use a human – in a covenant-based relationship – to carry out His plans.

God told a random guy named Abram to leave everything and go to a new land. God made an everlasting covenant with Abram. This covenant promised that in the new land, Abram would become a great nation. Why? God said, "[So] all the families on earth will be blessed through you."[1] Because of this promise, the world would start changing for the better. Abram obeyed and was renamed "Abraham"; sound familiar? His identity changed because of this new relationship.

God's covenant with Abraham was also unconditional. There was nothing Abraham did to deserve it, and there was nothing he could to do get out of it. The book of Hebrews tells us that it's impossible for God to lie; what He says WILL happen. So "Abraham waited patiently, and he received what God had promised."[2] We'll see the results of that promise as we continue through the Old Testament.

---

[1] *Genesis 12:3*   [2] *Hebrews 6:15*

For us living after Jesus, we have an amazing new perspective on this covenant: "For all of God's promises have been fulfilled in Christ with a resounding 'Yes!'"[1] The original promise was made to Abraham and his descendants, the Jews. Most of us are not Jewish, which means we are "Gentile" (you'll see that word a lot in the Bible.)

As a Gentile, "You did not know the covenant promises God had made to [Israel]. You lived in this world without God and without hope. But now you have been united with Christ Jesus. Once you were far away from God, but now you have been <u>brought near to Him</u> through the blood of Christ."[2] The separation has been repaired!

This is what the WHOLE Bible is getting to – this is the plan. God makes promises, and He keeps them. The result is you get to live in relationship with God, which is what your life was made for.

---

[1] *2 Corinthians 1:20* [2] *Ephesians 2:12-13*

READ & EXPLORE

Read Genesis 8:21-22. What does God promise Noah in these verses? [e]

God used Noah and Abraham to bring new life and blessing to the world. How can YOU bless someone else today?

Pray for the thing you wrote at the beginning of today's entry; God's promises are "yes" in Jesus, so ask your Father to help you.

DAY 9

MISSION IMPOSSIBLE

Start with prayer that the Holy Spirit will help you know Jesus more today.

Write down the things that are on the top of your mind today (the things that are taking up the most brain-space or mental energy):

```



```

We left off yesterday in Genesis 12 with the covenant God made with Abraham, where He promised to give Abraham land and innumerable descendants. What we didn't talk about yesterday was that when this promise was given, Abraham was a nonagenarian without any kids. Even though he saw no way for the promise to be fulfilled, he trusted God to fulfill His promise. And when he was 100 years old, his miracle baby, Isaac, was born.

Fast forward to Isaac's son, Jacob. Jacob's story is a soap opera of family dysfunction. He stole from his brother, lied to his dad on his deathbed, ran away from home, and ended up having 13 kids by four different women. Despite Jacob's outrageous life, God remembered the promise He made to Abraham, Jacob's grandfather. And God renewed Abraham's covenant with Jacob, promising to make him a great nation and to give him a homeland. God said to him,

"Your name is Jacob, but you will not be called Jacob any longer. From now on your name will be Israel."[1]

So from Jacob/Israel came the nation of Israelites, and it started with Jacob's 12 sons. Remember the story of Joseph and his coat of many colors? That's Jacob's son! Joseph ended up in Egypt because his mean older brothers sold him into slavery, but God used their treachery to save all of their lives. During a famine, Joseph was able to move his father and brothers to Egypt. They lived there happily for a long time and grew into a great nation of people. But after 400 years, the king of Egypt enslaved Jacob's big family (now the nation of Israel). The people cried out to God... and He heard their cry.

God appeared in a burning bush to a guy named Moses one day and said, "I am the God of your fathers—the God of Abraham, the God of Isaac, and the God of Jacob…The cry of the people of Israel has reached me, and I have seen how harshly the Egyptians abuse them. Now go, for I am sending you to Pharaoh. You must lead my people Israel out of Egypt."[2] God introduced Himself, reminded Moses of the covenant, and then laid out the plan: He was going to rescue the people, and Moses was going to do it. Once again, God partnered with a human to accomplish His plans.

So Moses headed back to Egypt and told Pharaoh to let God's people go. Pharaoh didn't want to, so God made his life pretty uncomfortable with 10 plagues. The plagues got worse and worse, but Pharaoh still didn't listen to God. Finally, the last plague killed the firstborn of every family in Egypt – except for the Israelites. Pharaoh finally relented, and the Israelites were free!

After traveling for a few days, they made camp by the Red Sea… only to see the Egyptian army come swooping around the corner to destroy them all! Pharaoh thought, "The Israelites are confused. They are trapped in the wilderness!"[3] The people looked up and watched their former oppressors riding in to completely destroy them all – men, women and children. And God had led them to a place with no way out. They were trapped. (Or so they thought.)

---

[1] *Genesis 35:10* [2] *Exodus 3:6, 9-10* [3] *Exodus 14:3*

But Moses told the people, "Do not be afraid. Stand still, and see the salvation of the Lord, which He will accomplish for you today."[1] In other words – "this looks impossible. But God can do more than you think." Moses stretched out his hand, and God parted the water so the people could cross the sea on dry ground. It was a miracle no one had expected.

God had not forgotten His people or His covenant with Abraham. He heard their cries and rescued them, because "the Lord is good, a strong refuge when trouble comes. He is close to those who trust in Him."[2] This is still true for you today! As God's child, He promises to hear your cry. And you can trust that "the Lord Himself will fight for you; you need only be still."[3]

---

[1] *Exodus 14:13 (NKJV)*   [3] *Exodus 14:14 (NIV)*
[2] *Nahum 1:7*

READ & EXPLORE

Read Philippians 4:6-7 and verse 19. What are we told to do in these verses?[f]

What does God promise us in these verses?[g]

Of those promises, which matters most to your story right now?

Write down your prayer today. Pray by thanking God for something, acknowledging His promises, and asking for help:

DAY 10

A PERSONAL RELATIONSHIP

Start with prayer.

What do YOU think God is like?

[blank box for writing]

God worked a miraculous rescue on behalf of His people, the Israelites. Hundreds of thousands of people were rescued from slavery because God keeps His promises. God's next task was to teach them about who He was and what He was like. Why? Because everyone has a perspective about God… and those perspectives aren't always true.

People during the time of the Exodus worshipped all sorts of false gods. The gods of the ancient religions were cruel and violent, impersonal, volatile beings. The people believed that if they could just appease the gods, then maybe the rains would come, the wild animals wouldn't attack, they'd have enough food. Their religions demanded unlimited sacrifices – including human sacrifice, in many cases – in exchange for protection from the elements. In the New

Testament, the apostle Paul explains that these false gods were actually demons in disguise![1] There is only one true God.

So when the Israelites were led out of Egypt by the God of their fathers (Abraham, Isaac, and Jacob), they were probably expecting a moody, temperamental, angry god they had to appease. God very quickly explained that He was not who they thought He was: "The Lord passed in front of Moses, calling out, 'Yahweh! The Lord! The God of compassion and mercy! I am slow to anger and filled with unfailing love and faithfulness. I lavish unfailing love to a thousand generations. I forgive iniquity, rebellion, and sin. But I do not excuse the guilty…'"[2]

So they learned that God's name is Yahweh, and His character is merciful. Compassionate. Patient. Loving. Faithful. He forgives, but He doesn't tolerate unchecked sin (i.e., He has healthy boundaries.)

What He described here is a relationship, just like the one He had with Abraham! Wait – a god who wants a relationship? All the other gods didn't want a relationship with humans beyond sacrifices. There was no concept of the gods "introducing" themselves; according to the common religions at the time, the gods just showed off what they could do, like making it rain or causing an earthquake, but they didn't want to be KNOWN. But Yahweh, the Lord, doesn't just show them His power – He reveals His heart. This God WANTS to be known by His creation.

This is how the God of the Bible is different than every other god or religious thought in the history of world religions: He is personal. He wants a relationship with humans, despite their brokenness, because He loves them like a Father.

And because He loves people, He made it clear that His people must never again worship any other gods. "Listen, O Israel!" He taught them. "The Lord is our God, the Lord alone. And you must love the Lord your God with all your heart, all your soul, and all your strength.[3] O Israel, stay away from idols! I am the one who answers your prayers and cares for you."[4] The Lord is the only God;

---

[1] 1 Cor. 10:19-20
[2] Exodus 34:6-7
[3] Deuteronomy 6:4-5
[4] Hosea 14:8

He absolutely loves His people. He wants His people's love in return.

Many people misunderstand God and think that He's moody and crabby, especially in the Old Testament. But people don't realize that the God in the Old Testament is the same in the New Testament; He never changes. He has always wanted to be known by us, and He has always wanted a relationship with us. Sending Jesus accomplished both of those things. If we want to know what God is like, we can look at Jesus, who "has revealed God to us."[1]

---

[1] *John 1:18*

READ & EXPLORE

Read the following verses and write down how they each describe God's character traits.[h]

Jonah 4:2 –

Psalm 86:15 –

Numbers 14:18 –

Joel 2:13 –

Why do you think this description is repeated so often throughout the Old Testament?

What does this mean for your story? How will this understanding change how you think, feel, or act?

Pray and thank God for His relationship with you and all the blessings He's given you, and ask Him for the things you need.

PART 2 RECAP

Congratulations on finishing your second week! We only covered two books in the Old Testament, because these books lay out the who, what, and where of the remaining 37 books. Next week, we'll do more of a birds-eye view of the storyline.

Where did the world (and humanity) come from, and how does that affect how you live your life?

What is the cause of all the pain, suffering, and death in the world?

What happened to humans' relationship with God because of sin, and what did He do about it?

What is a covenant, and how does the covenant with Abraham still affect us today?

What verse or concept has stood out to you or meant the most to you this week?

How has God blessed your life this week? What do you need prayer about in your life right now?

PART 3:

THE OLD COVENANT

Old Testament, Part 2

Human history
is the long terrible story
of man trying to find something other than God
which will make him happy.

C.S. Lewis

PART 3 INTRO

We cover a lot in Part 3! In Part 2, we studied Genesis and Exodus; now we'll look at the story in the rest of the books! My goal is to give you the perspective you need to understand God's story in the Old Testament. We've learned that God wants a relationship with the people He's created, but sin has separated humanity from Him. The Old Testament shows that He never gives up on reconciliation. It also points ahead to His ultimate rescue plan: Jesus!

Old Testament Overview

The Old Testament books tell the story of God's chosen people, the Israelites. The books here are listed according to their order in the story (not in the Bible's usual order).

Genesis **Exodus** **Leviticus** **Numbers**	God's perfect world was marred by sin, but He established covenantal relationships with His people in order to restore what was broken. He promised the land of Israel to Abraham's descendants, orchestrated their dramatic rescue from slavery, and then taught them how to be holy through the Law.
Deuteronomy **Joshua**	God reminded the people of the covenant terms and they moved into the Promised Land.

Judges **Ruth**	Despite the covenant, most of the People cycled into destructive patterns of sin... but some people stayed faithful!
1 & 2 Samuel	The people asked for a king to lead them. Eventually they get King David, who led them to follow the covenant and worship the Lord.
Job **Psalms** **Proverbs**	These are books of poetry and wisdom written at various times in the history of God's People.
Ecclesiastes **Song of Solomon**	Written by King Solomon, these books contain reflections on life and general wisdom for all.
1 & 2 Kings	A Temple was built in Jerusalem, but over time the people abandoned God repeatedly until they were kicked out of the Promised Land into exile.
Hosea Joel **Amos Obadiah** **Jonah Micah** **Nahum** **Habakkuk** **Zephaniah**	God sent these prophets before the exile (during 1 and 2 Kings) to deliver messages to His people.
Isaiah **Jeremiah** **Lamentations**	These prophets delivered God's messages while the Israelites were being evicted from the Promised Land into captivity and exile.
Ezekiel **Daniel**	These prophets wrote during exile about God's present and future plans, as well as their experiences in a foreign land.

1 & 2 Chronicles Ezra	As the exiles returned to the Promised Land to rebuild, Ezra wrote a review Israel's history, beginning with King David.
Nehemiah Esther	These are stories of captive Jews under Persian rule who courageously followed God's direction to protect their people.
Haggai Zechariah Malachi	These prophets wrote after exile to encourage the remnant. The last book in the Old Testament shows that though the people still sinned, a Redeemer was coming to save them.

DAY 11

SET APART

Start with prayer.

What do you think of when you hear the word "holy"?

Several weeks after the Israelites left Egypt, God made a formal invitation into another covenant. The first covenants in the Bible, the ones with Noah and Abraham, were unconditional promises of God. But unlike the covenants made with Noah and Abraham, this next covenant had two-way terms.

With Moses serving as a spokesman, the Lord laid out the terms of the covenant: "Give these instructions to the family of Jacob... If you will obey me and keep my covenant, you will be my own special treasure from among all the peoples on earth; for all the earth belongs to me."[1] This covenant built on Abraham's covenant – not only would Israel be a great nation, but also they would be set apart as God's special people on earth. When the people heard this, they

---

[1] *Exodus 19:3, 5*

liked how it sounded. "We will do everything the Lord has commanded,"[1] they said.

So God gave them the Ten Commandments. Don't worship other gods; don't make idols; honor the Sabbath. Don't lie, don't steal, don't kill. No envy. No sexual immorality. Honor your father and mother.

But after the Ten Commandments, there were a LOT of other laws. Laws about how to worship God. Laws about relationships. Laws about life in ancient times (like what happens if your ox gores someone with its horns, or if you find mildew in the walls of your house). God gave the people these laws for their good![2] They were surrounded by cultures with little to no sense of morality, hygiene, or social order, but God provided a blueprint for living a healthy life in that time period.

If the people followed those laws, they would be clearly different – set apart – from the cultures around them. And that was God's point. He said to the people, "You must be holy because I, the Lord your God, am holy."[3] Holy means "set apart" – God is different; therefore, they must be different, too. Their difference would show the world that the God of Israel is the only real God.

To remain faithful to the covenant, the people had to obey these laws. Think of it like a contract; you agree to pay your bill, and the provider gives you phone service. The people were given clear instructions. Obey God and be blessed. Or, choose to disobey, and you'll be cursed. These were the stipulations of the covenant. The heart of the Law is "to love the Lord your God, to walk in obedience to him, and keep his commands."[4] God made it very clear up front, though, that turning to worship other gods would result in destruction. The people agreed to these terms and "signed on the dotted line", so to speak.

Through the centuries, believers have made the mistake of looking at the Old Testament Law as God's idea of utopia or the perfect moral code – as though if you just were able to follow the Law, you'd be perfect, and you would be made right with God again. But

---

[1] *Exodus 19:8*
[2] *Deut.10:13*
[3] *Leviticus 19:2*
[4] *Deut. 30:16 (NIV)*

the apostle Paul, who spent most of his life studying the Law, said "it is clear that no one can be made right with God by trying to keep the law. For the Scriptures say, 'It is through faith that a righteous person has life.'"[1]

What does this mean for us today? It means that we need to keep context in mind when we read through the Old Testament laws. They were the stipulations of a covenant, and they were meant for the people's good. They also addressed a culture VERY different from ours.

The most important perspective for us, though, is that this covenant is now "obsolete" because of Jesus![2] We are no longer under Moses' covenant, so you don't have to observe the Law – or any other list of rules – to be right with God. Jesus started a New Covenant. If you believe in Jesus, your relationship with God is a permanent part of your identity. Because of Jesus, "nothing can ever separate us from God's love."[3]

---

[1] Galatians 3:11   [2] Hebrews 8:13   [3] Romans 8:38

READ & EXPLORE

Read Psalm 119:101-105. What is the writer's perspective on God's law (also called regulations, decrees, or commands)?[a]

What choices has the writer made? What has been the result of those choices?[b]

What does verse 105 mean to your story? How can you apply this truth to your life?

Your prayers for today:

DAY 12

THE SIN CYCLE

Start with prayer.

Have you ever made the same mistake over and over again? How did you get out of that cycle?

We're working our way through the Old Testament, and today we'll look at the books of Numbers, Joshua, and Judges. These books are the action stories of the Bible, full of gruesome stories of war, oppression, and corruption, but also stories of desperate heroism and faith.

To fully "get" these books, you have to remember the context. When the book of Numbers begins, the Israelites had just made a covenant with God that is outlined in the Old Testament Law. The Law explained the terms of the covenant (what the people had to do to remain in relationship with God). Obeying the law led to blessing; disobeying the law led to destruction. "I set before you life and death," God said. "Choose life!"[1] And the people signed on the dotted line.

As we'll see in Part 3, the people continually chose "death" instead of "life". The whole time you read it is one giant facepalm. God made things so clear; why didn't they just obey!? Well, because of sin! As the apostle Paul explains in the New Testament, sin "uses God's good commands for its own evil purposes."[2] God's law was GOOD, and its commands would lead to a better life, but people didn't always trust in God.

It started in the book of Numbers. Moses finally led the people to the land that God promised Abraham, but the people were too afraid to go in! After all the miracles God had done, and all of the good He promised them, they sat on their butts and complained …and ended up wandering in the desert.

The book of Joshua picks up the story 40 years later, when Moses was dead, and his apprentice, Joshua, led the people into the Land. Right away the people failed to consult the Lord with a major decision and chickened out when it came to obeying instructions. They found themselves trying to worship the one true God while sharing their Promised Land with people who worshiped evil false gods.

Everything went downhill from there. The book of Judges is filled with violence and destruction, because everyone (even the Judges who lead the people!) abandoned God's law and "did whatever seemed right in their own eyes."[3] Their sin resulted in destruction: enemies invaded and wrecked their way of life. They were slaves in their own land for many years, until they suddenly remembered their powerful God and cried out to Him for help. You think He'd just blow them off, since they'd blown Him off… but NO! In fact, it says "He was grieved by their misery."[4] God sent a rescuer (called a Judge) to save them. But when the judge died, the people "returned to their corrupt ways, behaving worse than those who had lived before them!"[5] This cycle happened over and over and over again:

---

[1] Deut.30:19 (NIV) [3] Judges 17:6 [5] Judges 2:19
[2] Romans 7:13 [4] Judges 10:16

1.) The people forgot God's goodness and worshipped false gods instead. 2.) They got oppressed and cried out for help. 3.) God rescued them. Then... back to step one: the people forgot God and worshipped false gods. They got oppressed and cried out for help. God rescued them. ... And on and on and on. Each time that they cycled back into worshipping other gods, society became worse and more corrupt than before. This is the train-wreck book of Judges.

After 13 cycles of this, the people said, "let's have a king instead!" The prophet Samuel was the last judge, and he was really frustrated by this request. The Lord told Samuel, "They don't want me to be their king any longer. Ever since I brought them from Egypt, they have continually abandoned me and followed other gods."[1] You can hear God's disappointment in these verses. Instead of a relationship, His people weren't even TRYING. The covenant was thrown by the wayside. But God did what they asked and appointed a king.

The first king of Israel was Saul, who started out following God, but even HE eventually did his own thing and didn't listen to instructions. And so, despite having a king, the cycle of sin continued.

We can learn a LOT from these stories, even though they are about a culture thousands of years ago that was very different from ours today. The human experience of sin and failure hasn't changed... but neither has God's faithfulness.

---

[1] *1 Samuel 8:7-8*

READ & EXPLORE

Read 1 Corinthians 10:13 and John 16:33. When we experience temptation, struggles, and pain, what can we hold on to?[c]

What does this mean for your story? How can you apply these truths to your life?

Your prayers for today:

DAY 13

IN GOOD TIMES AND BAD

Start with prayer.

What is your biggest "win" from this last week, and what was your greatest struggle?

Seek God, and your life improves; abandon God, and your life slowly falls apart. This is a thread that runs through the whole Bible, and it's true in my own experience, as well! If you think about it, nothing makes more sense. Sin separates us from our Creator, detaching us from our life's purpose. But the more we seek "the kingdom of God and His righteousness,"[1] the more we return to our original design, and the more things fall into place.

Few Bible stories give us a better example of this than the lives of the two greatest kings of Israel, David and Solomon. They both had times of seeking God, and both had times of abandoning Him. Their different responses to sin give us models to follow with our

---

[1] Matt. 6:33 (NKJV)

own struggle. (Today we'll look at David's story, and tomorrow we'll study Solomon.)

After Saul, Israel's first king, made a mess of things, the prophet Samuel anointed a random shepherd as the next king. God said, "I have found David son of Jesse, a man after my own heart. He will do everything I want him to do."[1]

David loved the Lord, and he worshiped Him in good times and in bad times. We have his worship recorded in

> ### FAMOUS LEADERS OF ISRAEL
>
> During the Exodus:
> - Moses
> - Joshua
>
> Period of the Judges:
> *12 total. Most famous ones:*
> - Deborah
> - Gideon
> - Samson
>
> United Kingdom of Israel:
> - King Saul
> - King David
> - King Solomon

Psalms, which is a book of prayer songs and praise to God. Most of the Psalms were written by David. They give us a model of how we can come to God with our whole heart and our whole life – both the good and the bad.

David celebrated good times by praising God: "How the king rejoices in your strength, O Lord! …With music and singing we celebrate your mighty acts."[2] David also came to God in times of great sorrow, shame, and fear. "Bend down, O Lord, and hear my prayer; answer me, for I need your help,"[3] he said. "You know of my shame, scorn, and disgrace… I am in despair."[4]

David came to his God at the highest points of his life and the lowest. When life was good, he thanked God! When life was uncertain and painful, he leaned on God's goodness and mercy. Because he lived his life whole-heartedly seeking God, the land of Israel entered into a time of great peace and prosperity.

Eventually, David was the recipient of another covenant with God. God promised to raise up a special king from David's family line. God told David, "I will raise up one of your descendants… and secure his throne forever. I will be his father, and he will be my son. I will never take my favor from him."[5] Hundreds of years later, this promise was fulfilled when Jesus came. Jesus was a descendant of

---

[1] *Acts 13:22*
[2] *Psalm 21:1, 13*
[3] *Psalm 86:1*
[4] *Psalm 69:19-20*
[5] *1 Chron. 17:11-13*

David, and He is now the King of a new nation of people who call on His name.

After describing this stand-up guy, you might be surprised to hear that at the peak of his rule, David turned away from God and started walking down the wrong path. He sinned horrifically – he knocked up some guy's wife, and then had the guy killed to keep it a secret!

Like all sin, David's had consequences: his family became very dysfunctional as time went on. But the important thing about David is that when someone confronted him about his sin, he **REPENTED**. When you "repent", you make a U-turn; you stop walking down the path you're on and jump back on the right one. In his sin, David turned **BACK** to God in deep sorrow about what he had done.

Sin leads to death, but seeking God always leads to life. In times of joy or sorrow – even in times of self-caused suffering – we can "come boldly to the throne of our gracious God. There we will receive His mercy, and we will find grace to help us when we need it most."[1]

---

[1] *Hebrews 4:16*

READ & EXPLORE

Read Psalm 51:1-2. David wrote this prayer after his big sin. What does he ask of God?[d] When have you felt like David did in this passage?

Now read 1 John 1:9. What promise are we given in this verse?[e]

What does this mean for your story? How can you apply this truth to your life?

Pray with confidence that God hears you. Thank God for all He has done for you and ask Him for what you need.

DAY 14

THE MOST EPIC TIME-OUT EVER

Start with prayer.

Have you ever made a poor choice or mistake that led to awful consequences? What happened?

David's son, Solomon, became the next king of Israel when David died. At first, he continued in his dad's ways, begging God, "Give me an understanding heart so that I can govern your people well and know the difference between right and wrong!"[1] God was so pleased with this request that He blessed Solomon with great prosperity and influence.

Solomon had the honor of building God a permanent house of worship. For hundreds of years, the people had been worshiping God in a portable tent called the Tabernacle. When his kingdom was established, Solomon spent seven years building a magnificent temple to the Lord in the city of Jerusalem. This became the central

---

[1] *1 Kings 3:9*

place of gathering for the Jewish people, and the one place God wanted His people to worship Him.

The Kingdom of Israel was at its peak; people worshiped God, Solomon's learning elevated the people, the nation prospered. Solomon was a prolific writer, and from him we got the wisdom books of Proverbs and Ecclesiastes, as well as Song of Solomon (his "song of songs, more wonderful than any other"[1]). But at the peak of his rule, when all was good, he forgot the Lord and turned to worship other gods. (Hmm… sound familiar?) This sin had consequences: after his death, the kingdom fell apart.

Starting in 1 Kings 12, the beautiful, thriving kingdom of Israel was split up into a southern kingdom (called Judah) and a northern kingdom (called Israel). Think Civil War – except in this case, it was two opposing kings tearing the country in half. The **northern kingdom** immediately abandoned the covenant by making idols to worship in more convenient locations instead of making the trek to God's Temple in Jerusalem. All the subsequent kings in the northern kingdom were evil, worshiping other gods and falling farther and farther away from the covenant relationship with the one true God.

The **southern kingdom**, on the other hand, still had the Temple in Jerusalem, serving as a constant reminder of the covenant. Some of the kings were good; they led the people in a renewal of the covenant, and worshiped God in the temple. Some of their kings were okay; they worshiped God, but didn't make all the people do it, too. Some of the kings were downright evil. "They followed all the pagan practices of the surrounding nations, desecrating the Temple of the Lord."[2]

After several hundred years of this mess, God called it. He sent foreign invaders into the Promised Land – and His people were kicked out. The northern kingdom, the one with all the evil kings, went first. A hundred-ish years later, the southern kingdom was captured, Solomon's beautiful temple was destroyed, and the people were taken into exile.

---

[1] *Song of Solomon 1:1*   [2] *2 Chron. 36:14*

Exile was basically one epically horrible time-out in the Babylonian Empire. In exile, God's people could no longer live in the land He had promised them. At the end of 2 Kings, the northern kingdom had been captured and dismantled, and the southern kingdom had been led into slavery in a foreign land. Remember – this is the consequence they agreed to in the Covenant! They promised to worship God only, and they failed to hold up their end of the deal. The result was ultimate destruction.

We've come a long way from the Garden of Eden when Adam and Eve first turned away from God. Sin continually hijacks the loving relationship God desires with His Creation! The Old Testament shows us that even when our hearts WANT to follow God, all of us "sin and fall short of the glory of God."[1] We are in desperate need of a Savior.

THE DIVIDED KINGDOM

The story in the books of 1 & 2 Kings goes back and forth between the northern and southern kingdoms. It helps to have a list of kings in front of you as you read to keep track of who is who. Here's a helpful guide to get you started:

King Solomon The last king of United Israel.	
Southern Kingdom (aka Judah)	Northern Kingdom (aka Israel)
King Rehoboam Solomon's son was the first king of Judah. After him, most kings were evil. Some were okay. Two or three were good.	King Jeroboam Solomon's servant was the first king of Israel. All kings after him were evil.
Conquered by Babylonian Empire (586 BC)	Conquered by Assyrian Empire (722 BC)

---

[1] Romans 3:23 (NIV)

READ & EXPLORE

Read Lamentations 3:19-25. This writer watched the exile happen and knew the destruction was deserved. But even though he was grieving, he didn't give up. According to this passage, what did he choose to hope in, and why?[f]

What is true about God, no matter what our current circumstances might look like?[g]

What situation in YOUR life seems beyond hope? What can you learn from this passage about your situation?

Write a prayer about this situation, and include the words from Lamentations 3:22-25.

BONUS: Praying Scripture like this over your life is a powerful and life-changing practice. As you learn the promises in Scripture and discover truths about God, work His words into your prayers. This helps you align your prayers with His will, remember truth in hard times, and rewrite your thoughts to be more like Jesus'.

DAY 15

REGRETS AND ROAD SIGNS

Start with prayer.

What's your biggest regret?

We all have regrets. Some are bigger and more devastating than others, but all leave you with the same "if only" feeling. If only I hadn't lost control; if only she hadn't gone down that street; if only he had known. Some regrets come from things completely out of my control, like when someone else's other poor choice led to unavoidable consequences. Some regrets, though, are my own fault, and those tend to be the worst. Especially when I knew better!

God's chosen people dealt with all kinds of regret when their kingdoms ended. The northern kingdom was conquered and forcibly assimilated into a pagan empire. Later, the southern kingdom was captured and led into slavery. "This disaster came upon the people of Israel because they worshipped other gods."[1]

---

[1] *2 Kings 17:7*

They'd made an agreement to worship the Lord ONLY, but they went back on their word. God placed a safe path before their feet, and they chose to step off the path into the sharp rocks and thorns. But God didn't abandon them. He sent messengers called prophets to serve as "road signs", so to speak, to get them back on the path.

The prophets spoke to the people on God's behalf. They're most famous for forecasting the end of time, but that's not all they did. Their purpose was to reveal God's heart and His plan. Here are some types of prophecies they made…

- **Prayers for God to remember His promises:** "O my God, lean down and listen to me. Open your eyes and see our despair. See how your city—the city that bears your name—lies in ruins. We make this plea, not because we deserve help, but because of your mercy."[1]
- **Helping the people reinterpret their current circumstances:** "Look at the proud! They trust in themselves, and their lives are crooked. But the righteous will live by their faithfulness to God."[2] (You think the proud are the successful ones, but really, success is having faith in God.)
- **Encouraging God's people to follow the covenant:** "Seek the Lord, all who are humble, and follow His commands. Seek to do what is right and to live humbly."[3]
- **Warning about sin's consequences; trying to get them to repent in time:** "'Repent, and turn from your sins. Don't let them destroy you! …For why should you die, O people of Israel? I don't want you to die,' says the Sovereign Lord. 'Turn back and live!'"[4]
- **Promising restoration of what they've lost:** "The exiles of Israel will return to their land… The captives from Jerusalem exiled in the north will return home."[5]
- **Helping the people to recognize the Messiah when He comes!** "But you, O Bethlehem Ephrathah, are only a small village among all the people of Judah. Yet a ruler of Israel …will come from you on My behalf."[6] (Jesus' birth was prophesied hundreds of years before it happened!)

---

[1] *Daniel 9:18*
[2] *Habakkuk 2:4*
[3] *Zephaniah 2:3*
[4] *Ezekiel 18:30-32*
[5] *Obadiah 1:20*
[6] *Micah 5:2*

The most important concepts we see in these messages are the mercy and love of God. This surprised me at first, because what I first noticed in these books are the violent consequences of sin. But when I read the books in context, what I saw is an all-powerful Creator God who's angry and heartbroken over His children's destructive choices.

He had every right to be angry, but God loved them enough to try and point them back on the right path. "Again and again the Lord had sent his prophets and seers to warn both Israel and Judah: 'Turn from all your evil ways. Obey my commands and decrees…' But the Israelites would not listen… They rejected His decrees and the covenant He had made with their ancestors, and they despised all his warnings.[1] They have been led astray by the same lies that deceived their ancestors."[2] When they were captured and exiled from the Promised Land, the people had known well in advance that it was coming – but they chose to ignore the warnings.

Talk about regret! If only they had listened! But even in exile, they were not beyond hope. God had not forgotten them, and He continued to promise restoration. This matters because it means that God hasn't forgotten YOU, either. Even with your biggest regret, there is power to restore what was lost.

THE PROPHETIC BOOKS

Remember – context is king! When you read the books of prophecy in the Old Testament, keep the writer, audience, and time period in mind.

Major Prophets – written by long-winded prophets before and during exile. (Isaiah, Jeremiah, Lamentations, Ezekiel, Daniel.)

Minor Prophets – shorter books written before & after exile.
- Written to northern kingdom: Hosea, Amos
- Written to southern kingdom: Joel, Habakkuk, Zephaniah, Micah
- Written to other nations: Obadiah, Jonah, Nahum
- Written after exile: Haggai, Zechariah, Malachi

---

[1] *2 Kings 17:13-15*   [2] *Amos 2:4*

READ & EXPLORE

Read Nehemiah 9:29-31. In this chapter, the remnant (Israelites who returned from exile) pray in remembrance of all that God has done. According to these verses, what was the people's sin?[h]

What was God's response to the people for all those years of rebellion? What does this passage show you about God's heart?[i]

When have you rebelled against God's instructions? What is His heart toward you as His child, even with that rebellion?

Because of Jesus, God will never abandon you, no matter how much you turn away. He is always wanting to help you and not to harm you. Write a prayer to Him below:

DAY 16

RESTORING THE REMNANT

Start with prayer.

What in your life seems "unfixable" right now?

Imagine for a minute that you just got kicked out of your house. Most living situations come with certain expectations – mortgage/rent payment, following house rules, taking care of your space. Just imagine you didn't follow those expectations, and you're on the street. How would you be feeling? (This may be a little too real for you; stay with me.)

Now imagine that feeling multiplied by total DESTRUCTION. You're not only kicked out, but everything is destroyed. Your home. Your church. Your nation. You'll never be going home again. Yikes! That's how what happened with God's people. They didn't follow the terms of the covenant. They REALLY blew it. Questions were probably rattling through their brains – Are we still God's people? Has God abandoned us? Can we ever have a relationship with Him?

"But this is what the Lord says: 'I would no more reject my people than I would change my laws that govern night and day, earth and sky. I will never abandon the descendants of Jacob or David...or change the plan that David's descendants will rule the descendants of Abraham, Isaac, and Jacob. Instead, I will restore them to their land and have mercy on them.'"[1]

He will never abandon His people. He won't change the plan just because they failed. INSTEAD, He will restore what they lost and have mercy on them in their shame. In other words – even when "we are unfaithful, He remains faithful, for He cannot deny who He is."[2] God is faithful to His promises, no matter how faithless we prove to be.

This promise of restoration came true. After 70 years in a foreign land, a remnant returned to the Promised Land and began to re-build. "Remnant" is an important word in the Old Testament. "Remnant" means "leftovers" or "what is left"; only SOME of the original amount. Not all of God's people came back.

The books of Ezra and Nehemiah (as well as parts of 1 & 2 Chronicles) tell us the story of this courageous group of people. They returned to rebuild Jerusalem and its wall, as well as the Temple of God so that proper worship could start again. The prophets Haggai and Zechariah wrote to encourage the people to stay committed, no matter how difficult and discouraging it might be.

Because it WAS discouraging. When they started rebuilding the Temple, "many of the older priests, Levites, and other leaders who had seen the first Temple wept aloud when they saw the new Temple's foundation."[3] There was no way they could return to the former splendor they'd experienced under King David and King Solomon.

But God said, "Does anyone remember this house—this Temple—in its former splendor? How, in comparison, does it look to you now? It must seem like nothing at all! But now the Lord says: ...Be strong, all you people still left in the land. And now get to work, for I am with you.[4] The Lord rejoices to see the work begin."[5] Returning from exile, rebuilding their lives, and recommitting to the

---

[1] *Jeremiah 33:25-26*   [3] *Ezra 3:12*   [5] *Zechariah 4:10*
[2] *2 Timothy 2:13*   [4] *Haggai 2:3-4*

covenant was a bittersweet time. Sin had consequences, but God was still with them!

Even then, they didn't always get it right. In fact, we learn from the last book of the Old Testament that they'd once again forgotten God and abandoned the covenant! "I am the Lord," He said, "And I do not change. That is why you descendants of Jacob are not already destroyed. Ever since the days of your ancestors, you have scorned my decrees and failed to obey them. Now return to me, and I will return to you."[1] Sin kept getting in the way, but God never gave up on them.

The whole Old Testament shows us that people can't do what it takes to have a relationship with God. Sin is not something we can fix. But God promises to do something about it. A promise of grace is woven all through the Old Testament, a thread that begins in Genesis and appears in every book, promising that Someone – a Redeemer – is coming to restore the relationship.

---

[1] *Malachi 3:6-7*

READ & EXPLORE

Read Jeremiah 31:33-34. What is the old covenant that God is talking about in this passage?[j]

According to this passage, how is the new covenant different than the old covenant?[k]

As a follower of Jesus, you are part of this covenant! What does this mean for you, according to this passage?

Prayers for today:

PART 3 RECAP

You are moving right along! We took a very zoomed-out view of the Old Testament storyline. People devote their lives to studying these books, but hopefully you've gained enough context to dive into these books on your own! Next week, we'll get to our favorite Person in the Bible: Jesus.

What is the point of the Old Testament Law? How should believers look at it today?

What does it mean to be holy? What did (and does!) that mean for God's people?

What do we know about God's heart for His people?

At the end of the Old Testament, what promises are God's people holding onto?

What has been the most meaningful concept that you've learned so far?

How has God blessed your life this week? What do you need prayer about in your life right now?

WHAT IS THE BIBLE?

PART 4:

JESUS

The New Testament, Part 1

I am a historian, I am not a believer,
but I must confess as a historian
that this penniless preacher from Nazareth
is irrevocably the very center of history.
Jesus Christ is easily
the most dominant figure in all history.

H.G. Wells

PART 4 INTRO

Now we're getting to the stories most of us know: the stories of Jesus! The best way to learn about Jesus is to read His stories for yourself, so you won't learn about all of the details from His life in the next two weeks. Instead, you'll learn some of the context and theology of the four Gospels (Matthew, Mark, Luke, and John) so you'll have a foundation as you read on your own.

The Books of the Bible

Books covered in Part 4 are underlined in the list below.

NEW TESTAMENT

GOSPELS
Matthew
Mark
Luke
John

HISTORY
Acts

EPISTLES
Romans
1 & 2 Corinthians
Galatians
Ephesians
Philippians
Colossians
1 & 2 Thessalonians
1 & 2 Timothy

Titus
Philemon
Hebrews
James
1 & 2 Peter
1 & 2 & 3 John
Jude

PROPHECY
Revelation

New Testament Overview

The New Testament books tell the story of God's plan of redemption for people everywhere. They are listed here according to what type of book they are.

Matthew **Mark** **Luke** **John**	The stories of Jesus told for four different reasons from four different perspectives.
Acts	This history book documents the initial growth of the Church.
Romans	A detailed explanation of the Gospel and how to live it out.
1 & 2 Corinthians **Galatians** **Philippians** **Ephesians** **Colossians** **1 & 2 Thessalonians**	Letters from the apostle Paul to the churches he started in various cities: Corinth, Galatia, Philippi, Ephesus, Colossae, and Thessalonica.
1 & 2 Timothy **Titus** **Philemon**	Letters from the apostle Paul to specific people.
Hebrews	An explanation of how Jesus fulfills Old Testament Law and what that means for believers today.
James **Jude**	Letters written by Jesus' half-brothers.
1 & 2 Peter	Letters written by the apostle Peter, one of Jesus' original 12 disciples.
1, 2, & 3 John	Three different letters all written by John, one of Jesus' closest friends and disciples.
Revelation	Letters to encourage and redirect the churches, and a vision of the end of time.

DAY 17

GOD IS WITH US

Start today with prayer.

Why does the Old Testament matter? After studying it, what do you think?

Let's do a quick recap of what we've studied in the Old Testament:

- God created humans and wanted a relationship with them.
- Humans sinned and were separated from God.
- God didn't give up on humanity. He set Israel apart and gave them the Law so they could be in a relationship with Him.
- Israel failed to live up to God's standard, but God still didn't give up; He promised a permanent solution.

We left off with the remnant back in the land of Israel, still falling away from the covenant God established. No matter how hard they tried, they couldn't make things right with God. They were slaves to sin.

In the midst of their failure, God made a promise to raise up someone in King David's line to break sin's power. "The day will come, says the Lord, when I will do for Israel and Judah all the good things I have promised them. In those days and at that time I will raise up a righteous descendant from King David's line. He will do what is just and right throughout the land. And this will be [His] name: 'The Lord Is Our Righteousness.'"[1]

"Righteousness" means "right-ness with God." Since we couldn't make ourselves right with God, the Lord Himself promised to come to do it for us. Then, the sin that entered the world with Adam and Eve would be undone, and we would finally have a right relationship with God again. "On that day the announcement to Jerusalem will be 'Cheer up, Zion! Don't be afraid! For the Lord your God is living among you. He is a mighty savior. He will take delight in you with gladness. With his love, he will calm all your fears.'"[2]

For 400 years after the Old Testament was written, God's people waited for that descendant – the One who would pave the way for God to live among His people again. Who would it be? They knew He would be a descendant of David, because of the covenant God made with King David, and there were also hundreds of other prophecies in the Old Testament that gave the people a rough idea of what to expect. And when Jesus came, He fulfilled every single one of the prophecies that described the promised Messiah (or "savior").

As you study the New Testament, you'll have a deeper and richer understanding of the Gospel because of your walk through the Old Testament. Because the story of Jesus didn't start in the Gospels – His story began before He was born. John 1:1 says, "in the beginning was the Word, and the Word was with God, and the Word was God."[3] What happened in the beginning? Oh yeah – "In the beginning God created the heavens and the earth."[4] This verse says that Jesus was actually there at Creation! In fact, "by Him all things were created."[5]

Read John 1:1 again, though: it says Jesus was WITH God, and He also WAS God. This verse describes the Trinity, an essential doctrine of Christianity. Scripture teaches us that God is one, but He is

---

[1] *Jeremiah 33:14-16*
[2] *Zephaniah 3:16-17*
[3] *John 1:1 (NKJV)*
[4] *Genesis 1:1*
[5] *Colossians 1:16*

also three: God the Father, God the Son (Jesus), and God the Holy Spirit. Stop and think about that until it bends your mind a little bit.

Throughout the centuries, Christians have tried to wrap their brains around how that works, but actually, we have to understand that our brains are too limited to fully understand the Trinity. God tells us in the book of Isaiah, "My ways are higher than your ways and my thoughts [are] higher than your thoughts."[1] In other words, God's nature is way beyond our finite human reasoning.

But this truth of a triune (three-in-one) God is crucial to the Christian faith, because it means that Jesus was both fully God AND fully human – which made His death the perfect sacrifice for our sins. "For, there is one God and one Mediator who can reconcile God and humanity – the man Christ Jesus."[2]

In Jesus, we have the solution to the problem of sin that has haunted humanity since the garden of Eden. God promised that "the virgin will… give birth to a son and will call him Immanuel, which means 'God with us.'[3] He will save the people from their sins."[4] Jesus was God Himself, which meant that He could fix what no human effort ever could – and the result is a restored relationship with our Creator.

[1] Isaiah 55:9
[2] 1 Timothy 2:5
[3] Isaiah 7:14
[4] Matthew 1:21

READ & EXPLORE

Read Hebrews 9:14. What did Jesus accomplish through His blood (meaning, His death on the cross)?[a]

According to this verse, how was the Trinity involved in this process?[b]

Thank Jesus for His sacrifice for you and ask Him for His strength today. Your prayers for today:

DAY 18

THAT ONE GUY FROM NAZARETH

Start with prayer.

Who is Jesus to you? Who do YOU say that He is?

Imagine that Facebook blows up one day about some random small-town nobody suddenly doing some really incredible things. A former quadriplegic is now running a marathon; mental illness stats are shrinking; a Happy Meal fed a whole stadium full of people, and when the alcohol ran out at a wedding, he turned tap water into the best wine anyone had ever tasted. And to top it all off, a little girl who died was brought back to life. Except it's not just clickbait – it's REAL.

There was no social media back in Jesus' day, but word still spread. Because in a culture with VERY limited scientific knowledge, suddenly you had a chance of healing a chronic illness. In a culture defined by political instability and religious exhaustion, you had a fresh reminder of God's mercy and love. Crowds gathered quickly.

When the crowds arrived, though, they found that Jesus offered much more than free food and a cool show. "Come to me," He'd say, "all of you who are weary and carry heavy burdens, and I will give you rest."[1] He looked people in the eyes. He held their babies. He visited the homes of social outcasts, giving respect and kindness to anyone and everyone. He promised to meet their deepest spiritual needs. "Those who drink the water I give will never be thirsty again," He said. "It becomes a fresh, bubbling spring within them, giving them eternal life."[2]

In the crowds there were still people who thought He was a fraud. One day Jesus was preaching in the synagogue (which is kind of like a local church), and at first, the people listening were startled by His confident teaching. But "then they scoffed, 'He's just a carpenter, the son of Mary and the brother of James, Joseph, Judas, and Simon. And his sisters live right here among us.' They were deeply offended and refused to believe in Him."[3] Basically – "this Jesus guy is just a normal dude! Who does he think he is?" For a long time, "even His brothers didn't believe in Him."[4]

All of these people were waiting for the Messiah to come. They thought they knew what to look for. The prophet Isaiah told them to expect someone who had "nothing beautiful or majestic about his appearance, nothing to attract us to him."[5] But even with all the prophecies and in all their dreaming and hoping for the promise of the Savior, they never expected someone like Jesus, with all His humility and radical love. So while many believed in Him, many also doubted. Some even rose up to oppose Him.

But even people's responses to Jesus had been prophesied. When Mary and Joseph brought their newborn Jesus to the Temple at 8 days old (because they were following the Old Testament Law) a faith-filled man named Simeon spoke these words over His life: "He is a light to reveal God to the nations, and He is the glory of your people Israel! …This child is destined to cause many in Israel to fall, and many others to rise. He has been sent as a sign from God, but many will oppose Him."[6] God knew, and even prepped Jesus' family, that His message wasn't always going to be well-received.

But Jesus never let opposition keep Him from obeying God's call on His life. He continued His ministry of teaching and comforting and healing and reconnecting lost people with God. We live like Christ

[1] Matthew 11:28
[2] John 4:14
[3] Mark 6:3
[4] John 7:5
[5] Isaiah 53:2
[6] Luke 2:32, 34

when we do the same. This is what it means to be "Christian"; Christian literally means "little Christ". As little Christs, we don't have to worry about how people see us. Our job is simply to follow Jesus and live by His example.

READ & EXPLORE

Read Luke 4:16-21. In this passage, Jesus gets to do the weekly Scripture reading for the people in His hometown. What does He mean in verse 21 when He says that these verses are fulfilled?[c] According to this passage, what did Jesus come to do?[d]

What does this mean for your relationship with Jesus today? How does this impact how you think or feel about who Jesus is?

Thank Jesus for coming to save you and ask Him to set you free in the way that you need:

BONUS QUESTION: In your Bible, there should be some sort of notation after verse 19, because the writer is quoting a different book in the Bible. The notation should lead you to a footnote with the reference of an Old Testament passage.

Find the original quote from the Old Testament! Write the reference below:

Why do you think it's so important that Jesus quoted THIS passage from the Old Testament?[e] *(Remember: context is king! What's happening around the passage?)*

DAY 19

THE UPSIDE-DOWN KINGDOM

Start with prayer.

What do you think it means to belong to God's Kingdom?

Very few kingdoms exist these days. But the word "kingdom" still evokes this image of a stately fellow in royal robes looking down his mustache at his subjects (I don't know why, but kings in my head have mustaches), sitting on a golden throne in a lofty stone hall. At least to me. Maybe you think of strength. Ruthlessness. Power. Competition, battle, swords. A survival-of-the-fittest, winner-takes-all mindset. As enticing as those descriptions might sound, all those things pale in comparison to God's kingdom.

The Kingdom of God (or the Kingdom of Heaven; the Gospels use both terms for the same thing) was Jesus' main subject when He preached. We learn from Jesus that the Kingdom of God is not an earthly kingdom that's maintained by human power and limited to a certain location or people. On the contrary: "The Kingdom of God can't be detected by visible signs," Jesus said. "You won't be able to say, 'Here it is!' or 'It's over there!' For the Kingdom of God is already among you.[1] It has come near to you!"[2]

This Kingdom is real and goes far beyond what we can experience with our earthly senses. Because of that, Jesus explained it with stories and word pictures (called parables). That's the same thing you and I do when we're teaching our kids something complex. "Why is the sky pink this morning?" my kid asks. It would go right over her head if I described how the level of molecules in the atmosphere refract light. Instead, I explain it in a way that makes sense to her. I tell her, "God painted the sky for you because He knows you like pink!" (Which is true; He's a good Dad, and He "has made everything beautiful in its time."[3])

In the same way, Jesus came to our level and told stories to help us understand. He said the Kingdom of God is like…

- A tiny mustard seed that grows into a huge tree[4]
- A man who unearthed a hidden treasure and gave up everything to get it[5]
- Fishermen who caught a ton of fish and threw the bad ones away[6]
- A king who forgave a great debt and expected his servant to do the same[7]
- A landowner hiring workers to tend his crops[8]
- A king who planned a great dinner party and got stood up by his whole guest list[9]

These are only a few examples; Jesus told many parables. When we look at the parables as small pieces of the whole picture, we start sensing how the Kingdom of God operates. We see that the Kingdom is both future and present reality for believers. Future – when God comes to establish His Kingdom at the end of this age of the world. Present – the Church (not your local weekly service, but the global crowd of Jesus-followers).

Why do these parables matter to us? Well, because they're talking about OUR present and OUR future. The Kingdom of God is

[1] Luke 17:20-21
[2] Luke 10:9 (NIV)
[3] Ecclesiastes 3:11
[4] Matthew 13:31-32
[5] Matthew 13:44
[6] Matthew 13:47-50
[7] Matthew 18:23-35
[8] Matthew 20:1-16
[9] Matthew 22:1-14

now, and it's at the end of time. This should encourage you! You're not just living life alone; you are part of a Kingdom.

But this Kingdom is not what most people expect – it's completely upside down. Instead of strength, Jesus says, "God blesses those who are poor and realize their need for Him."[1] Instead of wealth and excess, "God blesses those who hunger and thirst for justice."[2] Instead of power, Jesus says, "God blesses those who are humble... merciful... who work for peace."[3]

Jesus gently adjusts the expectations of the people away from what they expected from their Savior – power, wealth, success – and turns their eyes back to the truth that a heart earnestly seeking God has all it needs. That a life in tune with its Creator lives out its purpose. By doing this, He broke through all the tired human conventions and the crusty build-up of human effort and cut to the core of what matters most: "Seeking first the Kingdom of God and His righteousness."[4]

Let the Holy Spirit remind you of this truth today. Go back to the basics and remember that His kingdom is not necessarily what you expect it to look like – but it's much better.

---

[1] *Matthew 5:3*
[2] *Matthew 5:6*
[3] *Matthew 5:5, 7, 9*
[4] *Matt. 6:33 (NKJV)*

READ & EXPLORE

Read Luke 8:43-48. This woman's problem made her "unclean" in Jewish culture. By touching Jesus, she risked making Him "unclean", too. How do you think a normal King would react?

What does Jesus's response demonstrate about His Kingdom through His actions? What do you think this meant to the woman?f

How can you show that same love and compassion today?

Pray that God will give you an opportunity to be like Jesus to someone today:

DAY 20

THE HEART OF THE LAW

Pray to start your day.

What does it mean to follow Jesus?

```
[blank response box]
```

Jesus spent three years traveling around Israel, preaching about the Kingdom of God and meeting the needs of the people He encountered. Early in His ministry, He selected 12 men to be His students. These men came from many different walks of life; one was a right-wing political fanatic, a few were blue-collar fishermen, one was a white-collar tax collector. All of them left everything to become Jesus' disciples.

In those days, people who were well-studied in the Scriptures were called "rabbis", or "teachers". The rabbi's disciples, or followers, devoted their entire lives to being with the Rabbi. This was called "taking on the yoke" of the rabbi.

Rabbis would also teach in the synagogues to help people understand Scripture so they could live it out. At this time, the people only had the Old Testament as Scripture; they were living under the Old Covenant. Remember the covenant made through Moses way back in Exodus? It promised blessing for obedience and cursing for disobedience. Thousands of years after Moses, people were eager to follow the Law and gain the blessing of God.

Unfortunately, in their eagerness to obey, they lost track of God's heart and the point of the Law. A group of people called the Pharisees made it their life's mission to obey every single law in the Old Testament so that they could be right with God. They even added extra rules to help make sure they didn't disobey something on accident! For example, the Law says, "Observe the Sabbath, because it is holy to you;"[1] rest from all of your work. To make sure that they wouldn't disobey that law, they made long lists of what was "work" and what was not, and then forbade people from doing anything that even LOOKED like that type of work.

Maybe that sounds good in theory, but in practice, it actually PREVENTED them from following the Law. And, more importantly, it prevented them from walking with God in faith.

Parenting has helped me understand a little more of what this looks like. I want my kids to love each other; that's the heart of all of my rules. So I tell them things like, "Don't hit." Imagine that one of them, eager not to mess anything up, sat down and broke down exactly how to obey that rule: "Put your hands in your pockets when you're angry. Don't swing your hand out within 6 inches of another person…" The list could go on and on. Think of what it'd be like to live that way! You'd be worried all the time and paying far more attention to where your hands are than how to love your sibling, and eventually, your struggle to obey the LETTER of the law would lead you to disobey the HEART of the law. (For example, if you really love someone, you'd slap them to kill a mosquito, right?)

Now, Jesus was perfect. He obeyed God's law completely and didn't sin. But He completely blew off the Pharisees' extra rules, and they weren't pleased. "Look!" the Pharisees complained one day when the disciples were having a snack, "Your disciples are breaking the law by harvesting grain on the Sabbath!"[2] And, "Why [do] your disciples… eat without first performing the handwashing

---

[1] *Exodus 31:14 (NIV)*   [2] *Matthew 12:2*

ceremony?"[1] Because of these lapses, they assumed that Jesus was a false teacher leading people AWAY from following God's Law.

But Jesus had little patience for their nit-picky rules: "Hypocrites!" He said. "You are careful to tithe even the tiniest income from your herb gardens, but you ignore the more important aspects of the law – justice, mercy, and faith."[2] They'd mixed up their teachings with God's commands because they were determined to make themselves right with God.

This only caused them to miss the heart of the Law. Jesus said, "Isaiah was right when he prophesied about you, for he wrote, 'These people honor me with their lips, but their hearts are far from me. Their worship is a charade, for they teach man-made ideas as commands from God.'"[3] God has always been against a mindless following of rules without a relationship, and Jesus wanted to remind them of God's heart. He was always trying to point people away from self-righteousness and towards the righteousness that comes by faith. Why? Because self-righteousness only creates anxiety and exhaustion. Because of sin, we can NEVER make ourselves right with God. This is what Jesus meant when He taught, "Unless your righteousness is better than… the Pharisees, you will never enter the Kingdom of Heaven!"[4] In other words, even the Pharisees with all of their nit-picking and religious policing weren't good enough to get into heaven.

Why? Because throughout Scripture, "It is clear that no one can be made right with God by trying to keep the law. For the Scriptures say, 'It is through faith that a righteous person has life.'"[5] This is what Jesus taught to His disciples, and what we can rest in as His followers today: "since we have been made right in God's sight by faith, we have peace with God because of what Jesus Christ our Lord has done for us."[6]

---

[1] Mark 7:5
[2] Matthew 23:23
[3] Mark 7:6-7
[4] Matthew 5:20
[5] Galatians 3:11
[6] Romans 5:1

READ & EXPLORE

Read Matthew 11:28-29. What is Jesus's rabbinical yoke like?[g]

How does Jesus describe Himself in this passage?[h]

What is the result in our souls for following Jesus instead of the Law?[i] What do you think that means?

What rules have you been trying to follow to try and make sure God is happy with you? How can you submit those to Him today?

Pray that Jesus will help your soul to rest as you learn from Him.

DAY 21

THE DAY GOD MADE THINGS RIGHT

Start your day with prayer.

What is your favorite story of Jesus?

Most of us are familiar with the stories of Jesus, which is why in this book we have only looked at a couple major aspects of His ministry on earth. We could spend our whole lives exploring the books of Matthew, Mark, Luke, and John and still barely scratch the surface of who Jesus is. Even John says at the end of his book, "Jesus also did many other things. If they were all written down, I suppose the whole world could not contain the books that would be written."[1] In other words – "I had to pick only a few stories for you about Jesus, or we'd be here for the rest of our lives!"

The four Gospels are all a little different because each of them tells the story of Jesus from a different vantage point. They had different audiences in mind and different goals for writing their story.

_____

[1] *John 21:25*

- **Matthew** showed the Jewish people that Jesus was the Messiah.
- **Mark** showed Gentile believers that Jesus was a leader worth following.
- **Luke** did extensive research so that "you can be certain of the truth of everything you've been taught."[1]
- **John** wrote to everyone to explain that Jesus was not just a good human – that He was God incarnate.

For all their differences, though, each book took the time to explain the most important event of Jesus' life: His death and resurrection. This is the reason Jesus came to earth.

The Gospels record that when the time came, Jesus resolutely started for Jerusalem, knowing that He was going to suffer a violent death. If you've never read these books, you might be wondering why He was killed. Was it just a great big misunderstanding? Did He do something wrong?

The reason Jesus was sentenced to death was because of His words in John 10:30 – "I and the Father are one." He claimed to be God! So everyone who encountered Jesus had to make a choice: is He telling the truth, or not? You have to decide, too. Do you believe that this human is God, or do you believe that He's not? If He's not, He's either insane or evil. If He is, your whole existence and belief system needs to change.

Jesus preached a revolutionary message; He loved people and showed supernatural compassion; He performed amazing miracles; His life altered the course of history. He was an exemplary human. But even with all of that, you can't simply say, "He was a good man, but He was not God." He SAID He was God. So He either is who He said He was, or He's not (and if He's not, He's crazy or evil!).

The choice the loudest majority made back in Jesus' time was that He was NOT God. So Jesus was condemned to death on a cross. But this was God's plan all along (as we can see through Old Testament prophecy). For thousands of years, humanity's relationship with God was broken. It was "impossible to please God without faith"[2] because "all have sinned and fall short of the glory of God."[3]

---

[1] *Luke 1:4*   [2] *Hebrews 11:6*   [3] *Romans 3:23 (NIV)*

Even with God's patience and faithfulness, even with careful instructions via the Law, there was nothing humanity could do to fix that relationship.

So "at just the right time, when we were still powerless, Christ died for the ungodly."[1] When Jesus died, sin's power was broken, "for by the power of the eternal Spirit, Christ offered himself to God as a perfect sacrifice for our sins."[2] The mistake that Adam and Eve made way back in Genesis was fixed. Through Jesus, we can have a relationship with God again.

So now we can finish the verses that we've been looking at for several weeks now. We've read this verse many times: "For everyone has sinned; we all fall short of God's glorious standard." We've seen the effects of sin as we've gone through the Bible. Now, here's the rest of that passage:

"For everyone has sinned; we all fall short of God's glorious standard. But God, in His grace, freely makes us right in His sight. He did this through Jesus as the sacrifice for sin. People are made right with God when they believe that Jesus sacrificed His life, shedding His blood... We are made right with God by placing our faith in Jesus Christ."[3]

And this is the Gospel – the Good News. Believing in Jesus means you are made right with God. Everything you've learned so far has led up to this point. But this is only the beginning! Next week we'll look at the impact this event has on your life today.

---

[1] *Romans 5:6 (NIV)*   [2] *Hebrews 9:14*   [3] *Romans 3:24-25, 22*

READ & EXPLORE

Read Romans 5:15-16. What were the results of Adam's sin? How did that affect you?[j]

How did Jesus un-do those results? What is now possible because of Christ's sacrifice?[k]

Who in your life needs to know about this Good News?

Pray that these people would choose to believe in Jesus, and pray for an opportunity to share the Gospel with them:

PART 4 RECAP

Hooray! You're already through your 4th-ish week! Take a few minutes and review by yourself or with friends before moving on...

How does reading the Old Testament help us understand the New Testament?

What did Jesus mean by "The Kingdom of God"?

How do we know that Jesus is the promised Messiah?

What is the "Gospel" (or "Good News")?

What have you struggled with in your study so far? What would you like to know more about?

How has God blessed your life this week? What do you need prayer about in your life right now?

WHAT IS THE BIBLE?

PART 5:

THE NEW COVENANT

The New Testament, Part 2

Every person can know
the complete redemption of Jesus Christ,
a purpose for life, and a fullness of joy.
No, life won't ever be easy, but the trade-off
is a spin around Planet Earth
that actually means something.

Beth Moore

PART 5 INTRO

The books we study in Part 5 are all about embracing the truth of the Gospel. The book of Acts tells the story of the early church, and the remaining books are letters (called "epistles") written to the early believers. From these books, we learn how to live out our faith in a world still marred by sin – and we discover the joy of living in the New Covenant.

The Books of the Bible

Books covered in Part 5 are underlined in the list below.

NEW TESTAMENT

GOSPELS
Matthew
Mark
Luke
John

HISTORY
Acts

EPISTLES
Romans
1 & 2 Corinthians
Galatians
Ephesians
Philippians
Colossians
1 & 2 Thessalonians
1 & 2 Timothy

Titus
Philemon
Hebrews
James
1 & 2 Peter
1 & 2 & 3 John
Jude

PROPHECY
Revelation

DAY 22

THE CHURCH BEGINS

Start your day with prayer.

What do you think of when you hear the word "church"?

Jesus, the great Teacher, healer, friend, leader, was dead. Just imagine you're one of His twelve disciples for a minute. You'd followed this guy for three years, and you'd started to think He was the promised Messiah, and then suddenly He's gone! Imagine how devastated you'd be.

After Jesus was taken down from the cross and put in a tomb, His disciples went into hiding. For days they gathered and mourned for their fallen leader. Until the third day – when suddenly a bunch of women ran in and told them that Jesus' body was no longer in the tomb, and angels had said He was alive again! "But the story sounded like nonsense to the men, so they didn't believe it."[1]

Then Jesus showed up. ALIVE. With a real body. (He even ate a snack to prove it.)[2] Like the good Teacher He is, Jesus took the time

---

[1] *Luke 24:11*   [2] *Luke 24:43*

to explain what happened. "'When I was with you before,'" Jesus said, "'I told you that everything written about me in the law of Moses and the Prophets and in the Psalms must be fulfilled.' Then he opened their minds to understand the Scriptures."[1] Through the Old Testament, we understand what God's been up to, who Jesus was, why He came, and why He had to die.

When he taught his disciples one last time, Jesus gave them a mission: "Go and make disciples of all the nations, baptizing them in the name of the Father and the Son and the Holy Spirit. Teach these new disciples to obey all the commands I have given you."[2] And then He left. His last words were, "Stay in the city until the Holy Spirit comes and fills you with power from heaven."[3] In other words – "share the Good News... but not yet."

So this is where the book of Acts opens up. The disciples obeyed and didn't start fulfilling the mission Jesus gave them; they waited indefinitely for God to fill them with power like He promised.

And then, as they were praying one day, it happened. "Suddenly, there was a sound from heaven like the roaring of a mighty windstorm, and it filled the house where they were sitting. Then, what looked like flames or tongues of fire appeared and settled on each of them. And everyone present was filled with the Holy Spirit and began speaking in other languages."[4] A crowd gathered, wondering what the noise was all about. So Peter (one of Jesus' closest disciples) stepped up to explain, and he preached the Good News of Jesus for the very first time.

"Peter's words pierced their hearts, and they said to him and to the other apostles, 'Brothers, what should we do?' Peter replied, 'Each of you must repent of your sins and turn to God, and be baptized in the name of Jesus Christ for the forgiveness of your sins. Then you will receive the gift of the Holy Spirit.'"[5]

In that moment, 3,000 people made Jesus their Lord and Savior, and the Church was born.

The rest of the New Testament tells the story of the early growth of the Church, which Scripture calls the "Body of Christ."[6] When you

---

[1] Luke 24:44-45   [3] Luke 24:49   [5] Acts 2:37-38
[2] Matthew 28:19-20   [4] Acts 2:2-4   [6] Romans 12:5

hear "church", you might think of the building down the street with a steeple. But in Scripture, the Church is a group of people – any gathering of believers who share the same faith in Jesus.

That means YOU are a part of the Church. When you said "Yes" to Jesus like those first believers – when you repented, turned to God, and accepted Jesus for forgiveness of your sins – you were saved. Like those first Christians, you also received the gift of the Holy Spirit. Which means that believers today belong to that same Body that started 2,000 years ago, because "we have all been baptized into one body by one Spirit, and we all share the same Spirit."[1]

This means You are NOT alone in following Jesus or carrying out His mission! We'll talk more about this Good News over the next few days.

---

[1] *1 Cor. 12:13*

READ & EXPLORE

Read Ephesians 2:18-20. What can we do because of what Jesus did for us? (vs 18)[a]

What is our identity now because of Jesus? (Hint: look at phrases that begin with "you are")[b]

What two things make up the foundation of God's house? Who is the cornerstone? Why does that matter?[c]

How does this reading impact how you think, feel, or act?

Pray today that God would help you live as part of His body and by the power of the Spirit. Your prayers today:

WHAT IS THE BIBLE?

DAY 23

CHURCH MATTERS

Start today with prayer.

Do you think it's important to go to church every week? Why or why not?

```



```

Jesus established His Church when He sent the Holy Spirit on Pentecost. The 12 apostles (Jesus' original disciples, minus Judas) were filled with power to be His messengers,[1] and the Church grew exponentially. But if the Church is the global community of believers, how did we end up with the church(es) down the street? And why are so many churches so different? And if we are part of the Church simply by crossing the line of faith… why do we need to GO to a church?

To the very first Spirit-filled followers of Jesus, meeting together was a vital part of their faith. They worshiped together in the Jewish Temple in Jerusalem every day. They ate together regularly and listened hungrily to all the teaching that the apostles gave them. They wanted to learn all they could about Jesus! And the joy of their

---

[1] *Acts 1:8*

new faith was fulfilling and contagious – to the point that they freely gave away anything that could help someone else in God's family. Every day, more and more people chose to cross the line of faith.[1]

However, the religious leaders (remember the Pharisees?) were NOT pleased. They'd had Jesus killed, and now thousands of people believed the crazy story that He had come back to life! But despite public accusations and being sent to jail a few times, Peter and the apostles boldly proclaimed the truth of Jesus without fear "every day, in the Temple and from house to house."[2] The group of believers grew so rapidly that the original 12 apostles had to start training up more leaders. God blessed the sprouting church!

Then one day the growth changed. One of the new leaders, Stephen, was brought before the Jewish council to testify about the new faith in this Jesus. His speech made the religious leaders so angry that he was murdered on the spot! A great persecution of the early church began, and the new believers were scattered out of Jerusalem. They no longer could meet safely in public.

But once again, what looked like a blow to the baby church actually caused it to grow even faster. Despite the danger, "the believers who were scattered preached the Good News wherever they went."[3] It wasn't just the original 12 Apostles' job to "go and make disciples"[4] – it was EVERY BELIEVER'S job. And they took it seriously. The proof of their bold faith and obedience is found in your life and in my life. We heard the Gospel because of courageous believers throughout the centuries who lived out Jesus' mission.

These believers gave us a pattern for living the Christian life: Meet regularly together; learn about God together; become more like Jesus together. But then from that place of growth and unity, they are sent into the world to spread the Gospel no matter the risk.

We associate the word "church" more with a building in our culture, and that's not necessarily a bad thing. Buildings are gathering places, after all. But the church building is NOT the church; it represents the group of people who meet there regularly for growth and fellowship.

---

[1] Acts 2:42-47
[2] Acts 5:42
[3] Acts 8:4
[4] Matthew 28:19

The Christian life is not complete without the company of fellow Spirit-filled believers. Part of Jesus' mission to "make disciples" is engaging in a church community. The beauty is that all believers are at different points in their faith journeys. Some can walk alongside you as you follow Jesus together. Some might be further along in faith, so they can coach you in your journey. And YOU can help a younger believer (because you're always further along in faith than someone!)

If you don't currently have a church that you call "home", I encourage you to find a Bible-teaching church and plant yourself there. Why? Because "those who are planted in the house of the Lord shall flourish."[1] You are not alone in your faith (whether you like it or not!). You have millions of people who have gone before you, and you have millions alongside you now… and millions who can benefit from the lessons you've learned. You're part of the family now. Embrace it!

---

[1] Psalm 92:13 (NKJV)

READ & EXPLORE

Read Hebrews 10:23-25. The book of Hebrews was written to early believers who were facing intense persecution. What are we supposed to hold onto in struggles or hardships we experience?[d]

Why are we instructed to meet with each other?[e]

Have you "planted yourself" in the house of God? If so, how has the church blessed your faith? If not, what would it take for you to make that first step?

Pray that God will cause your faith to flourish as you invest in His people and His house. Your prayers today:

DAY 24

A NEW LIFE

Start today with prayer.

What's one thing about your past that you hope no one discovers?

There are all kinds of answers to that question. Secret addictions. Insecurities. Hidden trauma. Minor or major failures. (Or maybe like me you just hope no one finds any pictures of you from 9th grade.) But because you're human, chances are high that you've got something painful or shameful in your history. Most of us are terrified of our past realities coming out of the closet.

That's why I love the story of the apostle Paul. We know him as a faith hero who planted churches all over the known world, wrote most of the New Testament, and taught us the message of grace. That's not how he started out, though. We first meet Paul (also called Saul) in Acts 7, when Stephen was executed by the Jewish religious leaders. When the church scattered, Saul, a devout Pharisee, was the one spearheading the persecution. "He went from house to house, dragging out both men and women to throw them into prison.[1] He was eager to kill the Lord's followers."[2]

Then, as Saul rushed to another city, with legal permission to arrest more Christians, Jesus confronted him: "A light from heaven suddenly shone down around [Saul]. He fell to the ground and heard a voice saying to him, 'Saul! Saul! ...I am Jesus, the one you are persecuting. Now go into the city and you will be told what you must do.'"[3]

This encounter with Jesus left Saul/Paul blind. For three days, he waited – not eating or drinking – until an older Christian was sent to him. Paul's sight was restored, and immediately he was baptized. Mere days later he was in the Jewish synagogues teaching about Jesus!

Imagine Paul's situation for a minute. As a passionate Pharisee, he knew Old Testament Law and likely had much of it memorized. He thought he was serving God by stomping out a seemingly false teaching, only to find out that he had it all devastatingly wrong. It's likely that some of the Christians he befriended after his encounter with Jesus were related to people he'd thrown in jail (or even had killed.) Talk about shame and regret!

Yet this is also the man who wrote, "Now there is no condemnation for those who belong to Christ Jesus."[4] Paul no longer had any judgment or guilt for his horrible sin. Not because he was a psychopath who didn't recognize it as evil, but because "[Jesus] gave His life to free us from every kind of sin, to cleanse us, and to make us His very own people."[5] Believing in Jesus cleanses you before God and frees you from sin's hold on you – present or past.

Paul's baptism was a symbol of the cleansing he experienced. All Jesus-followers in the Bible participated in baptism (including Jesus Himself). In fact, we're commanded to "be baptized in the name of Jesus Christ for the forgiveness of our sins."[6] It's a physical act that reflects the spiritual act of dying to our old life – the dead life controlled by sin – and resurrecting to a new life led by the Holy Spirit.

---

[1] Acts 8:3   [3] Acts 9:3-6   [5] Titus 2:14
[2] Acts 9:1   [4] Romans 8:1   [6] Acts 2:38

"This means that anyone who belongs to Christ has become a new person," Paul explained. "The old life is gone; a new life has begun! And all of this is a gift from God, who brought us back to himself through Christ. And God has given us this task of reconciling people to him."[1] Paul's joy and gratitude for his encounter with Jesus led to innumerable saved lives. You and I are some of them.

And this is a beautiful testimony of how Jesus rescues us and makes us holy. If you've made Jesus your Lord and Savior, now "God is working in you, giving you the desire and the power to do what pleases Him,"[2] and we're empowered to bring the Gospel to the world – no matter what baggage our past contains.

We can have a right relationship with God because of Jesus' sacrifice. If you have given your life to Jesus, you are a new person. Have you been baptized to reflect that change? If not, call your home church and join the family!

---

[1] 2 Cor. 5:17-18   [2] Philippians 2:13

READ & EXPLORE

Read 1 Timothy 1:1-2. What type of writing is 1 Timothy, and what do you think the relationship between the writer and the recipient is like? How do you know?f

Now read 1 Timothy 1:12-14. What is Paul's attitude in these verses, and why?g

If you have given your life to Jesus, all your sin has been forgiven, just like Paul's. What is something that God has forgiven you for?

How have you changed since you gave your life to Jesus? What has it looked like for you to have "been made new"?

Pray and thank God for His wonderful forgiveness, and ask Him for power to "do what is right for the glory of God"[1]. Your prayers today:

If you want to get baptized, call your church and talk to a pastor!

---

[1] *Romans 6:13*

DAY 25

A NEW IDENTITY

Start your day with prayer.

What are your most defining characteristics?

From the very beginning of this book, we've talked about the purpose of humanity: to live in relationship with God. This relationship is the meaning of our existence. It's why we're created. When the first humans sinned, it marred our relationship with God. But now, because of Jesus, that first mistake is undone! "For Adam's sin led to condemnation, but God's free gift leads to our being made right with God, even though we are guilty of many sins."[1] And just like in the Old Testament, God wants to partner with us to accomplish His plans on the earth.

That's what we see in the rest of the New Testament. The book of Acts outlines how the Gospel spread "in Jerusalem, throughout Judea, in Samaria, and to the ends of the earth."[2] It spread like

---

[1] *Romans 5:16* [2] *Acts 1:8*

wildfire all over the known world as normal, every-day believers partnered with God to share the Good News about Jesus.

The new believers came from all walks of life. Many were Jews who recognized that Jesus was the Messiah. Others were Gentiles (non-Jewish people). They were everyone from foreign dignitaries[1] to high-ranking military officials[2], wealthy business owners like Lydia[3] to blue-collar workers like Priscilla and Aquilla.[4] Paul's famous words at this time were, "There is no longer Jew or Gentile, slave or free, male and female. For you are all one in Christ Jesus."[5] All other forms of identity are secondary to the fact that you now belong to Jesus.

The beautiful thing about the Church is that all of us are different, but we are also all united. Paul called this the Body of Christ. "The human body has many parts," he wrote, "but the many parts make up one whole body. So it is with the body of Christ. Some of us are Jews, some are Gentiles, some are slaves, and some are free. But we have all been baptized into one body by one Spirit, and we all share the same Spirit."[6] When you crossed the line of faith, the Holy Spirit moved in and has united you with Jesus-followers all over the world!

On top of that, the Holy Spirit has also given you special gifts. The skills, resources, and possessions you have are all gifts from God to bless yourself and others. But those natural gifts are only part of it – the Bible teaches that we each have a SUPERnatural gift, too! Some of us were given with supernatural faith; others have an above-average ability to teach or evangelize; some have special insight into situations; others can perform miracles. (See Romans 12 for more examples.)

If you aren't sure what your spiritual gift is, that's okay. Most people discover their gifts by using them. Start looking for ways to serve within your church using your natural skills. Look for ways to "put into action the generosity that comes from your faith:"[7] bless people with the resources you have (money, time, people, possessions,

---

[1] Acts 8
[2] Acts 10
[3] Acts 16
[4] Acts 18
[5] Galatians 3:28
[6] 1 Cor. 12:12-13
[7] Philemon 1:6

abilities). As you help others, you'll begin to develop and discover the gifts God has given you.

But just like those early Jesus-followers, keep your eyes on what matters most. The calling of every believer is to "'Love the Lord your God with all your heart, all your soul, all your strength, and all your mind.' And, 'Love your neighbor as yourself.'"[1] This is called the **Great Commandment** because it sums up everything written in the Old Testament – it's God's heart for us!

To be honest, I used to be really confused about the instruction to "Love God." I can't exactly love Him like I'd love another human – give Him a hug, for example, or make Him cookies. The Apostle John helped me understand what that looks like: "Love means doing what God has commanded us, and He has commanded us to love one another."[2] In other words, God's love language is obedience; His command is for us to love each other. When we love others, God receives it as love for Himself. (Jesus' parable in Matthew 25:34-40 gives a good illustration of this, too.)

We can live this out by following Jesus' instructions: "go and make disciples of all the nations, baptizing them in the name of the Father and the Son and the Holy Spirit. Teach these new disciples to obey all the commands I have given you."[3] This is the **Great Commission** – the final instructions for Jesus' followers. We make disciples by pointing everyone we meet back to Jesus: sharing our faith with people who don't know Him and encouraging fellow believers to continue seeking Him.

Your calling is to live out the Great Commandment and the Great Commission in unity with other believers, but also in your own unique way using all the unique things that God has given you. Discovering how YOU personally – in YOUR own special way, with YOUR own spiritual gifts – get to partner with God in His mission is one of the joys of the life of faith.

---

[1] Luke 10:27   [2] 2 John 1:6   [3] Matthew 28:19-20

READ & EXPLORE

Read Acts 2:42-47. These verses describe the birth of the church, when people first believed in Jesus and received the Holy Spirit. What do you notice about this church?[h]

What is one thing from this passage that you can start doing to build up the Body of Christ? What would it be like for you?

What gifts has God given you that you could use to bless people?

How does today's reading change your perspective of life as a follower of Jesus? How will that affect how you think, feel, or act?

Pray that God will lead you to opportunities today to use your gifts to bless others:

BONUS: Romans 12, Ephesians 4, or 1 Corinthians 12 to learn more about the different spiritual gifts that the Holy Spirit gives us.

DAY 26

A NEW COVENANT

What is grace?

The Gospel is the Good News of a New Covenant between God and humanity. The terms of this covenant are simply to accept Jesus as Lord and Savior. When this happens, we become a new creation;[1] we gain a relationship with God as "dearly loved children;"[2] we become "members of God's family";[3] we gain forgiveness and freedom.[4]

But living a life of faith is NOT always peaches and cream. Jesus tells us, "Here on earth you will have many trials and sorrows." Pain, suffering, struggle, and even persecution for what we believe is part of living in a broken world. "But take heart," Jesus says, "because I have overcome the world."[5]

Spoiler alert: Jesus is coming back to fix the world completely! When that happens, "God's home [will be] among His people! ...He will wipe every tear from their eyes, and there will be no more

---

[1] *2 Corinthians 5:17*
[2] *Ephesians 5:1 (NIV)*
[3] *Ephesians 2:19*
[4] *Colossians 1:13-14*
[5] *John 16:33*

death or sorrow or crying or pain."[1] The people who've chosen Jesus in this life will be with Him in the next life. The people who've rejected Jesus will end up in eternity without Him. Jesus is clear in all His teaching that anyone who does not cross the line of faith will spend eternity in hell. But Jesus is waiting with an open hand wanting to save every person, and all it takes is believing in Him!

But "how can they believe in him if they have never heard about Him? And how can they hear about him unless someone tells them?"[2] This is why the New Testament writers instruct us, implore us, to take up our cross and engage in Jesus' mission. It's the same mission that God has been carrying out from the very beginning: restoring a relationship with every human life. And like every Bible story, He carries out that mission through flawed humans: Noah. Moses. David. Solomon. Like Queen Esther, who trusted God and used her position to save thousands from destruction, "who knows whether YOU have come to the kingdom for such a time as this?"[3]

Now, living under the New Covenant, this mission has fallen to us. You've learned that we're called to live out the Great Commandment and the Great Commission. The New Testament letters teach us that to accomplish this mission, we need to stay connected into a local church. They tell us to live by the Spirit's power and not our own, using our gifts to bless people; they remind us that Jesus is coming back, and until then, to "take a firm stand… [and] keep a tight grip on what you were taught."[4]

What do we hold fast to? In short: GRACE. Grace is the heart of the New Covenant. We're not saved by the good things we do, by following a list of rules or having a good attitude. It's simple: "If you openly declare that Jesus is Lord and believe in your heart that God raised him from the dead, you will be saved."[5] We are saved by grace through faith in Jesus.[6] This is a free gift that we can't earn and can't be taken away. No matter what mistakes you make, under grace, you are always forgiven and in God's favor.

Now, that doesn't mean that we just can live however we want! Throughout church history, people have drastically misunderstood grace, saying, "God's marvelous grace allows us to live immoral

---

[1] *Revelation 21:3-4*
[2] *Romans 10:14*
[3] *Esther 4:14 (NKJV)*
[4] *2 Thess. 2:15 (MSG)*
[5] *Romans 10:9*
[6] *Ephesians 2:8-9*

lives!"[1] But the Bible is clear that "God's will is for [us] to be holy."[2] In fact, "those who do good prove that they are God's children."[3] Faith and holy living go hand in hand, because sin is still sin – it's wrong. What grace DOES mean is that "Sin is no longer your master... Instead, you live under the freedom of God's grace.[4] For God chose to save us through our Lord Jesus Christ, not to pour out His anger on us."[5] Under the Old Covenant, God's people disobeyed the law because sin controlled them. Now, you are set free from sin; God Himself is working in you to make you holy!

To be clear, this doesn't mean that we'll never struggle with sin again. Until Jesus comes back to completely fix the world, sin and pain and suffering are still a reality, and we're called to be holy despite all of that. But now, we live by the Spirit. No matter what mistakes we make, the Spirit lives in us and is guiding us to be more like Jesus.

Did you catch that? The Spirit of God is speaking to you. Regularly. Do you hear Him? It takes a little practice, but you CAN hear God talking to you. He speaks primarily through His Word, the Bible; sometimes He speaks through a small nudge in your heart. Many times He speaks through other believers. (It's not usually an audible voice from heaven, by the way.) The more you listen and obey, the more you recognize Him the next time He speaks. You become more and more like Christ as you listen to the Spirit.

But let's be honest; sometimes it's hard to live by the Spirit. Even Paul said that even though he knows the right things to do, he finds himself doing the wrong thing.[6] When it's hard to obey God, we can pray! Prayer "has great power and produces wonderful results."[7] What we don't want to do is start making a list of rules for ourselves. That's the trap the early church fell into; someone started falsely teaching them that to be a good Christian, they had to check off a to-do list (just like the Pharisees!). But we aren't under law anymore; we are under grace.

So now, "let us come boldly to the throne of our gracious God. There we will receive his mercy, and we will find grace to help us

---

[1] Jude 1:4

[2] 1 Thess. 4:3

[3] 3 John 1:11

[4] Romans 6:14

[5] 1 Thess. 5:9

[6] Romans 7:15

[7] James 5:16

when we need it most."[1] This is a promise we can claim with confidence. When we struggle with sin, when we experience trouble or hardship, we can come to God with confidence that He loves us no matter what we do, and He'll help us live the right way. That is the good news of grace.

---

[1] *Hebrews 4:16*

READ & EXPLORE

Read Galatians 5:22-23. What kind of results will we see in our lives when we follow the Spirit's leading?[i]

Which of these fruits do you want to see more of in your life right now? Why?

Pray and thank God for His grace and ask for help where you need it most. Ask Him to produce that fruit for you as you learn to follow the Spirit:

BONUS: Yesterday you prayed for an opportunity to bless someone. Did God give you a chance to do that? Write about it below!

PART 5 RECAP

You did it! You've worked your way through a study of the Bible! Fun fact: if you've stayed engaged all the way through to this point, you have read at least one verse from every single book of the Bible. That's quite a feat!

Part 5 will equip you with tools to continue studying on your own. Before you keep going, take some time to review Part 5 with a friend.

What did Jesus' death and resurrection accomplish for us? What symbolic practice represents this process?

What does it mean to live by the Spirit? What happens in our life when we do this?

What do we mean when we say we are under Grace and not Law?

What has impacted you the most from your reading this week? What have you struggled with in your study? What would you like to know more about?

How has God blessed your life this week? What do you need prayer about in your life right now?

PART 6:

NOW YOU TRY!

experiencing God's Word for yourself

The mark of spiritual maturity
is not how much you understand,
but how much you use.
In the spiritual realm, the opposite of ignorance
is not knowledge,
but obedience.

Howard G. Hendricks

PART 6 INTRO

We are down to our last four days of this study. You've come a long way already! You know that the Bible is the Word of God; you know the flow of the Old Testament stories; you know why Jesus came and how the Church began. But a vital part of living out your faith is engaging with God's word on your own!

Part 6 will equip you to read the Bible and get something out of it for yourself. The process you'll use is an acronym called PREP. Each day, you'll read a passage of Scripture and follow this acronym (with the help of some guiding questions!) to dig into a passage.

P.R.E.P

PRAY to start your time with God.	*Thank Him that He's always with you. Ask Him for wisdom as you read today.*
READ Scripture and reflect on it.	*What stands out to you? Why? Is anything confusing to you?*
EXPLORE what you've read.	*What does this passage teach you about God? About people? What situation, concept, or other Bible verse does this remind you of?*
PRACTICE what you've read as you go about your day.	*How can you live this out today? Who can you share this with?*

Study Options

You can choose one of two books to study for these final four days. Each day, you'll read study one chapter using PREP as a guide.

OPTION 1: JONAH. This Old Testament book paints a beautiful picture of God's heart for people.

OPTION 2: PHILIPPIANS. Paul wrote this letter to encourage and teach early Christians in the city of Philippi.

STUDY OPTION 1: JONAH

For the next four days, you'll be reading the story of Jonah, one of God's messengers in the Old Testament.

Most of God's messengers were sent to the Israelites, but Jonah was sent to a far-off place called Nineveh. This city was the source of every violent marauder, evil empire, and military takeover during this time period; they continually harassed Jonah's people.

But God had a redemption story even for people as evil as the Ninevites!

Day 27

GET UP AND GO!

PRAY. Thank God that He is always with you, and ask Him to give you wisdom as you read today:

READ. Read Jonah 1. Underline/highlight things that stand out to you as you read. Write question marks next to things that confuse you. You can also write notes in the margins of your Bible or jot them down in the space below.

EXPLORE. What does this passage teach you about God? What does it teach you about people? What situation, concept, or other Bible verse does this remind you of?

What did God tell Jonah to do? What happened when Jonah disobeyed God's orders? Where is he at the end of chapter 1?

Look at verses 14-16. What were the sailors feeling? What did they do when they couldn't save themselves? How did they respond to God's power?

What does this part of the story teach you about God's heart? Where do you see God's grace and mercy in this passage?

PRACTICE. How can you live this out today? Who can you share this with?

PRAY. Pray to launch your day from a foundation of God's Word. Ask Him to help you live out or understand what you read and thank Him for His presence.

Day 28

PRAYERS FROM A FISH

PRAY. Thank God that He is always with you, and ask Him to give you wisdom as you read today:

READ. Read Jonah 2. Underline/highlight things that stand out to you as you read. Write question marks next to things that confuse you. You can also write notes in the margins of your Bible or jot them down in the space below.

EXPLORE. What does this passage teach you about God? What does it teach you about people? What situation, concept, or other Bible verse does this remind you of?

Chapter 2 is Jonah's prayer to God while he sits alone in darkness. According to verse 2, what is Jonah celebrating in his prayer?

Read from verse 3 to the first half of verse 6, and put yourself in Jonah's shoes. How was he feeling, and how do you know?

In verse 7, Jonah tells us what he did right as his "life was slipping away". What did he do, and what was the result?

What have you learned from so far from the book of Jonah about the power of prayer?

PRACTICE. How can you live this out today? Who can you share this with?

PRAY. Pray to launch your day from a foundation of God's Word. Ask Him to help you live out or understand what you read and thank Him for His presence.

Day 29

CHANGE OF PLANS

> Since you've had some practice digging into Scripture, I'm starting to ask fewer guiding questions so you can find the important points on your own.

PRAY.

READ. Read Jonah 3.

EXPLORE. What does this passage teach you about God?

What does it teach you about people? What situation, concept, or other Bible verse does this remind you of?

What does the book of Jonah tell us about what Nineveh was like? With this context in mind, how are the events in Chapter 3 significant?

What do you learn about God's heart in this passage? Where else in the Bible has God responded in a similar way?

PRACTICE. How can you live this out today? Who can you share this with?

PRAY. Pray to launch your day from a foundation of God's Word. Ask Him to help you live out or understand what you read and thank Him for His presence.

Day 30
REALLY, GOD?

On your final day in this book, my guiding questions are gone, and you get to put into practice everything you've learned. Write down your thoughts as you PREP today's passage. Enjoy your time with Him today!

PRAY.

READ. Read Jonah 4.

EXPLORE.

PRACTICE.

PRAY. Pray to launch your day from a foundation of God's Word. Ask Him to help you live out or understand what you read and thank Him for His presence.

STUDY OPTION 2: PHILIPPIANS

For the next four days, we'll be reading Paul's letter to the church in Philippi. He wrote to encourage them and help them stand firm in faith. As Jesus-followers, Paul's words can encourage and instruct us, too! See what God has to say to YOU through the pages of this book.

Day 27
DEAR PHILIPPI...

PRAY. Thank God that He is always with you, and ask Him to give you wisdom as you read today:

READ. Read Philippians 1. Underline/highlight things that stand out to you as you read. Write question marks next to things that confuse you. You can also write notes in the margins of your Bible or jot them down in the space below.

EXPLORE. What does this passage teach you about God?

What does it teach you about people? What situation, concept, or other Bible verse does this remind you of?

In this passage, what does Paul teach us about following Jesus?

Look at verses 3-11. What does Paul pray over the people, and why?

Read verses 27-30. How does Paul tell the people to live? What does that mean for you as a Jesus-follower?

PRACTICE. How can you live this out today? Who can you share this with?

PRAY. Pray to launch your day from a foundation of God's Word. Ask Him to help you live out or understand what you read and thank Him for His presence.

Day 28
LIVE LIKE CHRIST!

PRAY. Thank God that He is always with you, and ask Him to give you wisdom as you read today:

READ. Read Philippians 2. Underline/highlight things that stand out to you as you read. Write question marks next to things that confuse you. You can also write notes in the margins of your Bible or jot them down in the space below.

EXPLORE. What does this passage teach you about God?

What does it teach you about people? What situation, concept, or other Bible verse does this remind you of?

Read verses 2-4 and 14-16. What instructions does Paul give Jesus-followers? How does he want them to interact with each other?

What attitude does Christ have in 2:5-11? What does Christ's example teach us?

What do we learn about Paul's assistants in verses 19-30?

PRACTICE. How can you live this out today? Who can you share this with?

PRAY. Pray to launch your day from a foundation of God's Word. Ask Him to help you live out or understand what you read and thank Him for His presence.

Day 29

FOLLOW MY EXAMPLE

Since you've had some practice digging into Scripture, I'm starting to ask fewer guiding questions so you can find the important points on your own.

PRAY.

READ. Read Philippians 3.

EXPLORE. What does this passage teach you about God? What does it teach you about people? What situation, concept, or other Bible verse does this remind you of?

What is Paul trying to teach the people in this passage?

What do you learn about Paul's heart for Christ and for the church?

How are we made right with God?

PRACTICE. How can you live this out today? Who can you share this with?

PRAY. Pray to launch your day from a foundation of God's Word. Ask Him to help you live out or understand what you read and thank Him for His presence.

Day 30
PRACTICE WHAT YOU LEARNED

On your final day in this book, my guiding questions are gone, and you get to put into practice everything you've learned. Write down your thoughts as you PREP today's passage. Enjoy your time with Him today!

PRAY.

READ. Read Philippians 4.

EXPLORE.

PRACTICE.

PRAY. Pray to launch your day from a foundation of God's Word. Ask Him to help you live out or understand what you read and thank Him for His presence.

PART 6 RECAP

PREP is a great way for you to engage in God's Word every day. You don't need to write in a journal to follow the process, although keeping a log of your prayers, Scripture reading, and aha! moments with God is helpful for seeing the pattern of His work in your life. There are lots of journaling apps you can use for this process.

It's also useful for Bible Studies with others! Gather a group of friends and use PREP to work through a book of the Bible. Try meeting regularly to talk about what you've learned, the questions you have, and the ways God has transformed you by His Word. Go to your local church to connect with other believers.

Today's review questions are designed to help propel you OUT of this book and into the next chapter of growing in knowledge of God.

How did this book go for you? How much were you able to read in a day? Do you enjoy the process of daily writing, or would you rather reflect out loud or on an app?

Who in your life could you meet with regularly to study your Bible?

What's next? What is God prompting you to start reading? Write the name of the book of the Bible or reading plan you'd like to begin tomorrow:

How has God blessed your life this week? What do you need prayer about in your life right now?

A Final Word

Congratulations! You've made it to the end! Statistically, you probably know more and have invested more in your faith now than most Christians. I'm not telling you this so your head inflates. I'm telling you this because the world is in dire need of whole-hearted believers to INVEST in the Kingdom of God – to follow Jesus' command to follow Him and make disciples.

"Go and make disciples" looks different for everyone. For some, it means secretly praying for coworkers and watching for an opportunity to talk about Jesus. For others, it means inviting hurting friends to church. Maybe it's handing out sandwiches and coats to people experiencing homelessness. Maybe it's pouring coffee for the weary people who show up at church on a weekend; maybe it's reading Bible stories to your kids at night. Maybe it's praying with people in the hospital, starting a Bible study at a coffee shop, or mentoring a struggling teen.

The point is that you can't keep your faith to yourself. You are responsible for what you know, and what you know is enough to help you and someone else experience the hope and salvation of Jesus.

And look at Matthew 28:20. What does Jesus promise? "I will be with you until the end of the age." Jesus – Immanuel – will never leave you.

This is our final chapter together. I may never meet you, but I end this book with a prayer for you and the people whose lives are transformed by your witness for Christ:

> *I ask God to give you complete knowledge of his will*
> *and to give you spiritual wisdom and understanding.*
> *Then the way you live will always honor and please the Lord,*
> *and your lives will produce every kind of good fruit.*
> *All the while, you will grow as you learn to know God better and better.*
> **Colossians 1:9-10**

Continue to follow Jesus. Spend daily time with Him in the Word. Pray throughout your day. Meet with other believers regularly and watch for opportunities to bless people. Your life will never be the same, because as you seek Him, you WILL find Him.

God bless!

Further Reading & Viewing

Want to know more about the things you've learned in *What is the Bible?* Check out these resources that I've found helpful in my own faith journey...

- *Seven Reasons Why We Can Trust the Bible* by Erwin Lutzer. (Chicago: Moody Publishers, 2015.)

- *Learn the Bible in 24 Hours* by Dr. Chuck Missler. (Nashville: Thomas Nelson, 2002.)

- "Run through the Bible: Part 1 – The Old Testament," by Pastor Ed Young. (YouTube video. November 4, 2018.)

- "Run through the Bible: Part 2 – The New Testament," by Pastor Ed Young. (YouTube video. November 11, 2018.)

- OverviewBible.com, a website by Jeffrey Krantz.

- *Mere Christianity* by C. S. Lewis. (New York: HarperCollins Publishers, 2001.)

- *The Case for a Creator* by Lee Strobel. (Grand Rapids: Zondervan, 2004.)

- *The Case for Christ* by Lee Strobel. (Grand Rapids: Zondervan, 1998.)

Acknowledgments

Over the course of my life, God has surrounded me with wise and godly people who have shaped my story. I'm overwhelmingly grateful for the investment they've made in my spiritual walk.

To my husband, David, who has been pushing me to write since he found out I could, and never let me give up on that dream.

To my parents, John and Peg, who trained me in life and in faith. Thank you for teaching me about Jesus and showing me the joy of learning.

To my pastors, Eric and Kelly. Thank you for your guidance and influence and trust.

To the many teachers and pastors who helped me to understand faith and to follow Jesus: Jane Boehler, Summer Sipes, Ragan Ewing, Vanessta Spark, Pastor Bob Kosbau, Pastor Wayne Braudrick, and Pastor Britney Ahlmann. The seeds you planted in my life have led to the creation of this book. Thank you for sharing your faith.

To my church family at Free Grace United, and especially my students: you're a living example of God's love and power. Thank you for the lessons you've taught me over the years.

And, more than anyone else, "All praise to God, the Father of our Lord Jesus Christ." (1 Peter 1:3)

The Answers in the Back of the Book

Understanding the Bible comes with time and takes practice. But then I first started reading the Bible on my own, I was always nervous that I was reading it wrong. What if I made a mistake? How would I even know if I misunderstood something?

I have good news – you aren't alone in studying your Bible! Jesus has given us two things to help us understand Scripture:

1. **The Holy Spirit!** Every believer has the Holy Spirit living in them, and He "guides us into all truth".[1]
2. **The Church!** Jesus developed the church to help believers grow up and stand firm in faith. Jesus-followers are commanded to "teach and counsel each other with all the wisdom God gives."[2] When you're stuck on something in the Bible, talk about it with another Jesus-follower who is a little further along in faith!

I included my own answers to the questions in each entry so that you can see the thoughts of another Jesus-follower as you work through the book. Over time, my hope is that you'll lean into the Holy Spirit and the believers around you as you dig into Scripture, and you won't need to look my answers anymore.

---

[1] John 16:13   [2] Colossians 3:16

PART 1

ᵃ (Day 0) When we seek God and put our trust in Him, we lack for no good thing.

ᵃ (Day 1) God loved YOU so much that He sent Jesus to die for you. Because of that sacrifice, you can have eternal life – meaning, a life fully lived in God's presence now and even after you physically die.

ᵇ Teaching, rebuking, correcting, and training in righteousness.

ᶜ He was appointed as a prophet to the nations, meaning that God was going to use him to deliver messages to the people.

ᵈ He felt totally unqualified; he was too young! He felt that God chose the wrong person.

ᵉ God tells him not to deny the calling; God will be with him. What he feels like is impossible is possible because God will be with him and will protect him.

ᶠ They are witnesses to the life of faith – meaning that they give us an example that living a life of faith is worth it! This matters to us because we know that other people have gone before us in faith; we're not alone in our struggle.

ᵍ Strip off weights that slow us down – distractions, etc., and especially sin that trips us when we run. And run with endurance with our eyes on Jesus.

ʰ He calmed himself down, and now his soul is like a "weaned" child (a baby who can feed itself and doesn't need a bottle.) In other words, his soul is quiet and at rest, not worried about what it needs.

ⁱ Look at verse 1; he is not dwelling on things that are too big for him to understand. Verse 1 and 2 together are saying that instead of freaking out about his questions, he is at rest because of verse 3 – put your hope in the Lord!

ʲ Don't freak out when you don't get your questions answered! Hope in God.

PART 2

ᵃ We are God's masterpiece! He planned things for us to do long ago, and now we're made new because of Jesus.

ᵇ He made us new in Jesus. Because of sin, we couldn't do the good things He planned for us, but now because of Jesus, we can!

ᶜ We produce fruit when we remain in Jesus. Just like a branch can't be productive if it's cut off from the vine, we can't be productive if we're cut off from Jesus. "Fruit" is another word for "results". You can look at Galatians 5:22-23 for a list of results that happen naturally when we stay connected to Jesus!

ᵈ Jesus says to remain in His love. When we obey Jesus' commandment, we remain in His love. His commandment is to love each other! (verse 13)

ᵉ The world will never again be destroyed by water, no matter how evil things get. He also promises that as long as the earth exists, we'll still experience the seasons and time. In other words, the earth will keep rotating and revolving around the sun!

ᶠ We are told not to be anxious, but to pray over everything that worries us.

ᵍ God promises to guard our hearts and minds with His peace. He also promises to supply ALL of our needs.

ʰ Merciful and compassionate, slow to get angry (patient) and filled with unfailing love.

PART 3

ᵃ God's words are like honey to him. They give him understanding so he knows the truth; it guides him in life.

ᵇ He refused to walk on an evil path so he can stay obedient; he has been taught well by God's regulations. They give him understanding on the right way of life.

ᶜ When we are tempted to sin, God will give us a way out. And we will experience trouble of all kinds, but Jesus has overcome the world! We're not alone in our struggles.

ᵈ He asked God to have mercy on him, because God is filled with unfailing love. He asked God to be compassionate and to cleanse him of his sin.

ᵉ When we confess our sin to God, He forgives our sins! He cleanses us from all unrighteousness. When you confessed your sins in the moment that you made Jesus your forgiver and leader, your sin was completely forgiven and you were cleansed forever.

ᶠ He chooses to hope in the Lord because His mercy is new every day. His love is unfailing.

ᵍ God's faithful love never ends; He always loves us, no matter what we're going through. We get a fresh start every day with Him. He is faithful no matter how much we abandon Him, and He always shows up when we look for Him.

ʰ They became proud and stubbornly disobeyed God's commands. They turned their backs on Him and refused to listen.

ⁱ He was loving and patient with them, warning them by His Spirit through the prophets. Eventually He let them be conquered, but He protected them from being totally wiped out. Basically, He allows natural consequences for sins but patiently waits for people to come back.

ʲ The Mosaic Covenant – the covenant made through Moses. It's the if/then covenant – if you obey, then you'll be blessed; disobey, and then you'll be cursed.

ᵏ The Law will be written on their hearts. Instead of having to offer regular sacrifices for their sins, God will forgive their sin and forget it forever.

PART 4

ᵃ The blood of Christ purifies us from sin so we can worship God!

ᵇ Jesus offered Himself to God the Father as a sacrifice for sins through the power of the Holy Spirit.

ᶜ It means that He is the one this passage is talking about! He's come to set captives free, bring sight to the blind, proclaim liberty to the oppressed.

ᵈ He's been sent to share the Good News with people. We know that the Good News is a new way to be made right with God through faith in Jesus! Because of Jesus, the spiritually blind will see and captives will be set free

ᵉ If you read the context of this passage in Isaiah, you can see that it's talking about the promised Messiah. So Jesus is claiming that He's here not just to set people free, but that He's the One they've been waiting for all this time!

ᶠ He shows compassion and love for her. He even calls her "daughter"! He welcomes her into a family instead of treating her like an outcast.

ᵍ His yoke is easy and His burden is light, unlike that of the Pharisees.

ʰ He is humble and gentle at heart! We want to learn from someone like that!

ⁱ We find rest for our souls! Imagine what it's like to know you're loved no matter what you do. Following Jesus means you are dearly loved by God no matter how you act.

ʲ Adam's sin caused death in all humanity. That's true for humans today, too; we're destined to die because of that one man's mistake.

ᵏ Jesus's sacrifice brought life! When we choose to believe in Him, we receive a free gift of righteousness and we win over sin and death.

PART 5

ᵃ We can all come to the Father through the Holy Spirit because of what Christ has done! This means that our relationship with God is restored!

ᵇ We are citizens in God's kingdom; we are members of God's family; we are His household.

ᶜ The foundation is the prophets and apostles – and those words are found in Scripture! The cornerstone, or what keeps everything in line with the truth, is Jesus. The reason this is important is that our faith is founded in Jesus and in Scripture alone.

ᵈ We can hold tightly to our hope in Jesus. When we die, we go to be with Him because we've chosen to have faith in what He's done for us.

ᵉ To motivate each other to do good works (or to be like Jesus!) and to encourage each other in faith.

ᶠ 1 Timothy is a letter from the apostle Paul to a guy named Timothy. It sounds like a close, spiritual father/son relationship, because Paul calls him a "true son in the faith", and then Paul prays that Timothy will have grace, mercy, and peace.

ᵍ You can tell that he feels grateful and overwhelmed by God's goodness. He tells Timothy about his past and all of the good things that God has done for him.

ʰ They felt awe. The Apostles did miracles. They all met together and were generous with each other. They sounded unified and joyful. They praised God all of the time and people were being saved daily.

ⁱ When we say "yes" to the Spirit's leading and choose to obey God, we are planting a seed that eventually produces love, joy, peace, patience, kindness, goodness, faithfulness, gentleness, and self-control

www.ingramcontent.com/pod-product-compliance
Lightning Source LLC
LaVergne TN
LVHW052023080426
835513LV00018B/2131